LEADER GUIDE

TO HAVE & TO HOLD

PREPARING FOR A GODLY MARRIAGE

BYRON & CARLA WEATHERSBEE

LifeWay Press® Nashville, Tennessee

Published by LifeWay Press® • ©2017 Byron and Carla Weathersbee

ISBN 978-1-4300-6356-8
Item 005791140
Dewey decimal classification: 306.81
Subject heading: MARRIAGE \ DOMESTIC RELATIONS \ MARRIAGE COUNSELING

To order additional copies of this resource, write LifeWay Church Resources Customer Service; One LifeWay Plaza; Nashville, TN 37234-0113; FAX order to 615.251.5933; call toll-free 800.458.2772; email orderentry@lifeway.com; order online at LifeWay.com; or visit the LifeWay Christian Store serving you.

Printed in the United States of America.
Adult Ministry Publishing, LifeWay Church Resources,
One LifeWay Plaza, Nashville, TN 37234-0152

CONTENTS

DR. BYRON *and* CARLA WEATHERSBEE

Byron and Carla Weathersbee serve as the Executive Directors of Summers Mill Retreat and Conference Center in Salado, Texas. In addition, they lead Legacy Family Ministries, a ministry they co-founded in 1995. Legacy's mission is to pass on biblical principles from one generation to the next by providing marriage preparation for pre-engaged and engaged couples. Byron and Carla authored *Before Forever: How do you know that you know?*—a book for seriously dating couples.

Carla currently leads the women's ministry at their church, and Byron serves as an Elder. Byron has served on church staff, as a university chaplain, and recently as the vice president for student life at the University of Mary Hardin-Baylor.

Both Byron and Carla are graduates of Baylor University. Carla has done graduate work in exercise physiology and Byron earned his doctoral degree in leadership from The Southern Baptist Theological Seminary and a Master's degree from Southwestern Baptist Theological Seminary.

Carla and Byron live in Salado, Texas, and have been married for over thirty years. They have three grown children. Recently, two of their children were married.

CREATING AN EXPERIENCE:
GETTING STARTED

> "I'll go anywhere with God, as long as it is forward."[1]
> **DAVID LIVINGSTONE**

In America, the average money, time, and energy spent on a wedding is astronomical. According to The Knot's 2016 *Real Weddings Study*, in a survey of nearly thirteen thousand couples, the average price of a wedding was $35,329, up eight percent from 2015. The biggest expense was the venue, $16,107,[2] followed by the engagement ring, $6,163, and photography/videography, $4,778. The smallest expense on the list was the $100 typically spent on wedding day makeup.[3] While thousands of dollars are spent for the wedding day, little, if any, money, time, and energy are spent in preparation for the marriage itself.

In helping prepare couples for their special wedding day, may you be challenged to allow Almighty God to work powerfully in the lives of the couple as the Holy Spirit mysteriously brings about oneness. In the days ahead, both the leaders and couples attending will need to be empowered by something greater than themselves. Allow God to be teacher, instructor, guide, counselor, and coach as you help couples discover biblical principles that govern the way life can be lived to the fullest. Remember: a good instructor teaches people, not simply material.

DIFFERENT APPROACH TO PREMARITAL COUNSELING
To Have and To Hold offers a different approach to "premarital counseling." We like to think of ourselves as marriage educators rather than counselors. Through preventive education, we believe couples can be equipped to avoid divorce and build smart marriages and healthy families. In preparing this course, we have taken into account couples' busy schedules, the importance of interaction, and the need for a simplified lifestyle during the engagement season.

BUSY SCHEDULES

The days prior to a wedding can be busy and hectic. We have attempted to maximize the study time by giving couples important information in a simplified and condensed version—an outline version of sorts. One of the biggest mistakes many couples make is that of collecting great resources and then becoming overwhelmed by the amount of information gathered. Oftentimes, resources are put on the "I'll get to that later" shelf, only to be pulled down during a major crisis several years later—often too little, too late—when the damage is done.

To Have and To Hold takes advantage of couples' leisure time—*yeah right, what leisure time?* The time when they are not sleeping, eating, working, going to school, planning a wedding, or other non-negotiable times set into their schedules. Of course, a couple will need to discipline themselves to get the most out of this study, but we have created weekly activities that allow them to capitalize on their time together. They will make time for each other; why not use it positively to work through the issues vital to a healthy lifelong relationship?

INTERACTIVE

Each week the couples will be given four to five prep activities concerning that session's topic. Couples will be encouraged to meditate on a Scripture passage, do a biblical word study, go to a romantic place, or do some other activity to creatively challenge their thinking. These assignments are not a major time commitment, but they are vital as a couple works through issues.

Some of the weekly prep activities are designed to be fun, creative, and light. Remember, it is okay for couples to relax, laugh, and escape from the wedding plans for awhile. Finding a balanced approach will help couples gain insight during the more fast-paced days.

To Have and To Hold's ultimate goal is for the couple to interact, discuss, and possibly debate the subject matter. We believe it is better for couples to discuss their thoughts, ideals, fears, and questions rather than simply read the latest resource regarding an issue. We encourage you, leader, to creatively adapt each session to meet your needs and the needs of your couples as you journey through the Bible study book. Remember: interaction and communication are key as you help couples seek God's principles for a fulfilling marriage.

The *To Have and To Hold* Bible study book is designed to guide couples through the following structure:

- **Attend the introductory session, if in a group.**

- **Intro and Prep Work of the next session**—The Intro section of each week introduces a marriage topic along with the biblical principles that apply to that topic or part of the vows. Then couples are challenged to explore their understanding of these concepts and practically apply those biblical guidelines to their own relationships.

- **Driving Questions**—At the next group meeting, these questions guide the conversation. Note: the questions throughout this Leader Guide are for you, as the leader, to ask of the couple (or couples) to kick off discussion.

- **Synopsis**—Conclude each session here to reinforce the content you've been discussing.

This rhythm is repeated for each session until completion.

MAKE IT PERSONAL

The Leader Guide will assist you in developing your marriage preparation course. However, it was not written as a "Quick Lesson Approach" to leading a marriage preparation session/class. Please be innovative and creative. Remember to make it personal. This needs to be a grassroots movement where you meet the needs of your community of influence.

PRACTICAL AND SIMPLE

Few people enjoy reading long, complicated, technical manuals. Thus, our attempt to challenge thinking is simplistic and practical. The curriculum is not intended to be a comprehensive, in-depth, "all-answer" resource. Instead, we hope to equip couples with some basic tools that are as old as time. Oftentimes the simplistic principles are easy to understand but complicated to live out. As you, the leader, work through each section, the ultimate teacher, the Holy Spirit, will help in practical ways to implement the biblical principles you present. As you build a foundation, it is important to begin with the basics and then build on what you know. The focus of *To Have and To Hold* is life change—practical and simple life change.

GETTING STARTED

Before you, as the leader, get started, you will need to understand a few more things.

- Most sections parallel parts of the traditional marriage vows and the study concludes with keys to living out those vows.

- The focus is not on the Bible study book or leader/teacher but on the learning process that God is bringing to their lives. We hope the Holy Spirit will be your instructor. However, couples love hearing stories from your own marriage.

FINAL THOUGHTS

A strong Christian marriage provides a foundation for generations to come. Be real, honest, and transparent as you lead these couples in marriage preparation. The church needs leaders who will work hard, invest much, pray often, and love abundantly. The return on your investment will be huge. As the couple whom you have guided meets at the altar, may they be adequately prepared to fulfill the marital vows—and enjoy the process. Have fun! The best is yet to come.

HELPFUL TIPS

- Make this study yours. Invest time in preparing. Consistently refine your teaching plan each time you lead a group.

- The first time you lead a couple or group through this study will be the most labor intensive.

- You are creating an experience, not just passing information along.

- Remember you teach couples; you *do not* teach curriculum. Personal relationships are the key.

TOOLS

We'd like to provide you with as many tools and illustrations as possible as you lead couple(s) through this journey. We'll include suggested illustrations at the end of each session. We've also put some tools in the appendix in the back of the Leader Guide; you can find additional tools online at LifeWay.com/ToHaveAndToHold. As you begin, you may find these resources particularly helpful:

- Consent to Premarital Education (See Figure 1 in the appendix.)

- Clergy and/or Counselor Permission (See Figure 2 in the appendix.)

- Optional Introductory Meeting—ideal for retreat and small or large group settings. (See the appendix.)

Dear Leader,

Discipling a couple as they learn how to navigate marriage is a sacred privilege. We want you to customize your teaching plan. Although we have provided thought-provoking discussion questions, illustrations, and learning activities, our hope is that you will provide the muscle and personality around the skeletal structure in this Leader Guide. It is important to open each session with an icebreaker question that references participants' Prep Work answers in the Bible study book. This provides accountability and encouragement for them to continue working through those assignments. Please allow the couple(s) to express their thoughts, opinions, and questions. Remember, God is not intimidated by our questions. In fact, a question that seems off the wall may lead a couple to discover truths about God that could not be known in any other way. Remember to pray specifically that the Holy Spirit will be the instructor. God desires to give a correct opinion of Himself through marriage. In the process, we learn to love others. We are thankful for your investment.

Byron and Carla Weathersbee

THE PURPOSE
for MARRIAGE

WHY AM I GETTING MARRIED?

OVERVIEW

The purpose of this section is to help you understand the biblical foundation for marriage. Marriage is an earthly picture of a divine institution. Thus, your marriage has the potential to glorify God and to provide an example to the world of what God's home will be like. Our hope is for you to establish a firm spiritual foundation upon which to build your lives and your marriage.

> *"A good marriage is not finding the right person so much as it is being the right person."*[1]
> **STEPHEN CROTTS**

"I TAKE THEE TO BE MY WEDDED WIFE/HUSBAND"

"... they are no longer two, but one."
MATTHEW 19:6

SESSION GOAL

To understand God's biblical foundation and purpose for marriage in order to establish a theological foundation that provides stability and oneness in the marital relationship.

KEY BIBLICAL PRINCIPLES

- Genesis 1:26-27; Ephesians 5:31-33—Humans mirror God's image uniquely in marriage.
- Genesis 1:28a—Families are to multiply a godly heritage.
- Genesis 2:18—God intends marriage for partners to experience companionship and to complement each other.
- Deuteronomy 6:1-12; Psalm 78:3-8; Mathew 28:19-20; 2 Timothy 2:2—God intends marriage for partners to evangelize and disciple the world by passing on a legacy to children.

Dear Leader,
This may be the first time you've met with this couple. Be sure they each have their Bible study books. They should read through the first session and complete the Prep Work before you meet together for Session 1. Together, you'll work through the Driving Questions and then the Synopsis provided following the session. If doing this study in a group environment, we encourage you to use the optional introductory meeting we've provided in the appendix (p. 165). Thank you again for your investment in the next generation of marriages and godly families.

I (Carla) will never forget the feeling of seeing my last bridesmaid walk down the aisle, leaving only me and my dad. The moment I had anticipated for a lifetime was finally here. I wanted our wedding to be more than a mere formality. I wanted to soak in every moment and every detail. My dad was silent and calm as usual. Yet, I could sense how proud and happy he was to present me to the man with whom I was to spend the rest of my life.

When my dad placed my hand in Byron's hand, calmness and assurance replaced my anxiety. I knew without a doubt that this moment was right. I had never been so sure of a decision in all my life. That hot summer day we began the process of two becoming one. I took Byron to become part of me—all of me.

LIVING OUT THE VOWS

Three children (one of which had childhood cancer), twelve moves in five cities, and thirty-plus years of ministry later, I now realize how crucial it is to grasp God's purpose and plan for marriage. During our engagement, my expectations of marriage reflected reasonable and God-given desires. I wanted companionship, affection, and someone with whom to share life. However, oftentimes my motives for pursuing these desires were self-centered. Unfortunately, too many couples enter marriage with a consumer mentality, each person focusing on his or her own happiness rather than that of his or her partner. We are, instead, to enter into a loving covenant, considering the other as more important than self.

UNDERSTANDING THE PURPOSE

Most engaged couples come to their wedding day with hopes of a satisfying companionship. Why, then, do many excited newlyweds lose their hopes and allow isolation to replace oneness? Neither spouse feels loved, respected, or understood. Boredom replaces romance. Wonder turns to a wandering relationship. One thing I have learned: good marriages require work, commitment, and laughter.

As your journey begins, our desire is to help you establish a firm spiritual foundation. Take time to prepare by working through the questions behind the question, "Why am I getting married?"

How did working through the Bible study book go this week?

STARTER QUESTIONS FROM THE BIBLE STUDY BOOK WILL LEAD INTO THE SESSION.

What are some reasons why you want to marry?

What are you most excited about regarding your upcoming marriage?

In what ways are you and your (future) spouse similar? Different?

Name one fear you have about getting married.

TRANSITIONAL QUESTION: What was your definition of marriage?

STATE THE PART OF THE VOWS AND PRESENT THE KEY QUESTION (P. 11) FOR THIS SECTION.

PRAY.

DRIVING QUESTIONS
(40 minutes)

WHAT DO YOU EXPECT TO GET OUT OF MARRIAGE?

What are some expectations you have for your marriage?

Our expectations often dictate our direction for marriage. How?

What needs do you hope are met?

HELPFUL TIP: *Our hope is to spur conversation and discussion between the couple. Do not feel as if you have to cover all of the details in a section.*

Our expectations often dictate our direction in marriage. Honestly, most couples are entering marriage to have their needs met regarding affection, companionship, family, and financial security. Some may have the need to leave home. Many of these expectations reflect reasonable God-given desires. However, when we pursue these desires with shortsighted strategies and motives, we'll run into problems.

Illustration: Compass—True North vs. Magnetic North
(See The Tools, p. 22.)

"You must know for which harbor you are headed if you are to catch the right wind to get you there."[2]

SENECA

What are some of God's expectations for marriage?

God's expectations for marriage include:
- *Sanctification: Marriage will change us for the better.*
- *Servanthood: Marriage enables us to serve someone else.*
- *Spiritual growth: Marriage places us under the mutual spirit of love.*
- *Model: Christians need to see marriage as a picture of Christ's relationship to the church.*

WHY ENTER A MARRIAGE COVENANT?

Read Genesis 2:15-25. What is Adam's dilemma?

What is God's solution?

Go back to the beginning, where God initiated marriage in Genesis 2:15-25. Adam's dilemma (Gen. 2:18a) was that God believed, "It is not good for man to be alone." Therefore, God provided a solution (Gen. 2:18b) by stating, "I will make a helper suitable for him." Therefore, God designed oneness in Genesis 2:24 (NASB): "For this reason a man shall leave his father and his mother, and be joined to his wife; and they shall become one flesh." Basically this means that marital oneness is in agreement with God's will and purpose.

What are some challenges to maintaining oneness?

How are a covenant and a contract similar? Different?

Remind the couple(s) that there is a difference between a covenant and a contract. A contractual agreement can easily be canceled or adapted by the signing of names and is simply legally binding. A marriage covenant, however, is both spiritually and legally binding.[3] "A covenant calls for the binding of hearts."[4]

A covenant implies that a couple is being spiritually glued together where nothing but death could separate. This kind of agreement involves a lifetime commitment.

Covenant literally means "cutting [or] passing between pieces of flesh."[5] The Hebrew word picture was the joining of flesh, hearts being meshed, sacrifice being made.

"Too many couples enter marriage blinded by unrealistic expectations. They believe a high level of continuous romantic love should characterize the relationship. As one young adult said, 'I wanted marriage to fulfill all my desires. I needed security, someone to take care of me, intellectual stimulation, and economic security immediately—but it just wasn't that.' People are looking for something 'magical' to happen in marriage. But magic doesn't make a marriage work: hard work does."[6]

H. NORMAN WRIGHT

WHY DOES DISILLUSIONMENT COME WHEN THE HONEYMOON IS OVER?

It is important for couples to have realistic expectations. When the honeymoon is over, if the couple is not prepared, disillusionment can destroy a marriage.

H. Norman Wright says, "I think that almost everyone who marries eventually experiences some degree of disillusionment ... it's usually an increased awareness that the relationship isn't going as well as expected."[7]

How does a newly married couple establish realistic expectations for the first few years of marriage?

What can a couple do to prepare for the disillusionment phase?

During the early days of marriage, couples bare all and see all for the first time. The closeness that comes with intimacy exposes our hearts and often unearths our own selfishness. It is easy to give in to the sinful nature. Reality sets in, and unfortunately, it often looks different from what was originally expected.

HOW CAN DISILLUSIONMENT LEAD TO FULFILLMENT AND SATISFACTION?

How do we find freedom from the expectations of others?

Longtime marriage and communication expert Gary Smalley said, "The more we place our expectations on another person, the more control we give them over our emotional and spiritual state. The freer we are of expectations from others—and the more we depend upon God alone—the more pure and honest our love for others will become."[8]

To keep couples from losing hope and becoming discouraged, leaders need to help them learn how to allow their relationships with God to become a source of marital fulfillment.

In addition, couples need to be taught that Mr. or Mrs. Right is not a superhero nor a savior. A person cannot and will not meet all our needs. Unfortunately, we will let one another down no matter how hard we try. Leaders need to help couples learn to accept Mr. or Mrs. Right for who he or she is as a person. A couple should not marry with the intent to change one another.

"Don't marry someone who has characteristics that you feel are intolerable."[9]

DR. JAMES DOBSON

Ask couples to list a few ways to keep from losing hope and becoming discouraged during the disillusionment phase.

What can be learned from times when we let one another down?

As marriage educators, our job is objectively to help the couples purposefully move away from unrealistic expectations and grow in understanding the truth about themselves, their mates, and their marriages. It is such a privilege and honor to be married. Help couples understand this high calling.

Hopefully we can help them live out Psalm 62:1,5 that says, "Truly my soul finds rest in God; my salvation comes from him…Yes, my soul, find rest in God; my hope comes from him."

SYNOPSIS

"Strong families hold the key to a strong society...because every other institution in society is predicated on and dependent upon strong families. And you can't have strong families without God as the centerpiece of the marriage union that ties that family together."[10]

DR. TONY EVANS

God's purposes for marriage are much higher and greater than our own. In Genesis 2:18 God said "It is not good for the man to be alone," and He created Eve as an answer to that aloneness. Even though Adam had a perfect relationship with God, a perfect environment, and all of the possessions he wanted, there was still a void of intimacy. Blending two individuals into oneness was the divine goal. Adam and Eve were made to become suitable counterparts who could balance and back one another in every way.

TWO BECOME ONE FOR A REASON.

In all of life's struggles, pain, and disappointment, you will need each other's companionship and intimacy. This intimacy develops from an attitude of servanthood in seeking to meet each other's needs and desires.

One can only have this attitude as one realizes that his or her ultimate well-being depends on God and not fully on a spouse. Only when I allow my relationship with God to be the most important relationship in my life can I find a sense of security, fulfillment, and satisfaction that does not depend on my husband's response. I can love Byron out of the love I receive from Christ and then use that love to help meet needs in his life.

God ordained marriage to be an earthly picture of the relationship between Christ and the church. Jesus Christ's love for the church, according to Ephesians 5, is sacrificial and unconditional. He laid down His life to present the church, His bride, whole and complete. Likewise, when a husband and wife love each other as they do their own bodies, nurturing and caring for each other, they live out the beautiful picture of Christ's oneness with the church.

The task of developing oneness will probably be one of the most challenging jobs you will face. Apart from a personal relationship with Jesus Christ, oneness in your marriage will never be fully realized. After all, it was God who created marriage for our well-being. Therefore, His plans, purposes, and ways can be trusted.

GOD'S PURPOSES ARE BIGGER THAN ANY WEDDING CEREMONY.

Even in the midst of God's plan, marriage is not easy. Life's disappointments and irritations combined with our own self-centeredness remind us of how much we need a Savior. It makes sense that so many marriages fail in America. Christ is not central for most couples and a consumer view of marriage is the norm; therefore, self-centeredness erodes intimacy and companionship. Without Christ, the vows promised at the altar can never be fully realized.

The key to a healthy marriage is for each of us to focus on becoming the person God created us to become. As author David Egner states, "The issue is not just what our Lord says about marriage. Solutions are found by discovering what He has said about basic issues of faith and character and then applying those perspectives to the seasons of marriage."[11]

In various ways, we are daily reminded of the first part of our marriage vows, "I take thee to be my wedded wife/husband." As we journey through the next seven sessions, our hope is for you to fully appreciate the significance of these powerful words. What an incredible privilege to be married!

THE TOOLS

COMPASS ILLUSTRATION:
TRUE NORTH VS. MAGNETIC NORTH

True north is the North Pole. "It's a fixed position that never changes." Maps are drawn from true north. "A compass . . . does not point to true north. Rather, it points to a magnetic field that is located roughly 1,300 miles away from the North Pole. This is called 'Magnetic North.' Every pilot and every sea captain must make constant adjustments from what a *compass* says is north and what the *map* says is true north. Failing to make this adjustments of even a few degrees early in the journey could mean missing the destination by hundreds of miles."[12]

- *True north = God's Word ("fixed, certain and absolute"[13])*
- *Magnetic north = "Can be deceiving; Looks right. . .feels right, yet it will not direct you to your desired destination"[14]*

Challenge couples to chart their spiritual journeys (both individually and together) by the true north of God's Word. Guide them to reflect on and ask God to reveal who or what they have allowed to guide them thus far. Talk through practical ways they can intentionally build their lives and marriages on biblical principles.

NOTES

ROLES *and* RESPONSIBILITIES

WHAT'S MY PART?

OVERVIEW

The purpose of this section is to clarify, establish, and help you understand the biblical functions of a husband and a wife within marriage. These biblical principles are designed by God to provide order in the family so that there is freedom and security as we carry out the responsibilities of life.

"Self-centered individuality destroys oneness and companionship."

"... TO HAVE AND TO HOLD FROM THIS DAY FORWARD."

"A marriage may be made in heaven, but the maintenance must be done on earth."[1]
RICHARD EXLEY

SESSION GOAL

Following God's principles leads to oneness and freedom in the roles and responsibilities of husband and wife.

KEY BIBLICAL PRINCIPLES

- Genesis 2:18—Aloneness is not good, thus the creation of a helper.
- Genesis 2:18—Being a helper is a primary role for the wife.
- Mark 10:42-45—Servant leadership is modeled by Jesus.
- Ephesians 5—Learn to imitate Christ in the husband and wife relationship. Our ultimate role is to love as Christ loved.
- Ephesians 5:23—Headship is a primary role for the husband.

Dear Leader,

We've found when people rebel against husband and wife roles they are often actually arguing against traditional stereotypes. Usually the traditional, stereotypical "responsibilities" are quite different from biblically prescribed roles. We make a simple distinction between roles and responsibilities. In this section, you as the leader will attempt to help couples understand a value standard that comes from God and distinguish between biblical values and our cultural norms. True biblical principles provide structure, order, and function in the home. These principles will transcend time, philosophy, and ethnicity. True biblical principles, established by our holy God, worked in 1955, 1255, and will still be relevant for generations to come.

As we get started, be sure to read through the Considerations— Framework for Discussion on the following page. We want engaged couples to ask two simple yet profound questions:

1. What is my part?

2. How can I contribute to making order and oneness in our family so there is freedom and security as we carry out life's responsibilities?

We pray your discussion will not become bogged down in the "submission dispute" and miss God's design for an effective husband and wife team.

HELPFUL TIP: *This section may prove difficult due to varying biblical interpretation. Be respectful of each person's view and consult the additional commentary below to help in preparation.*

CONSIDERATIONS—FRAMEWORK FOR DISCUSSION

As you prepare, please keep in mind the following marital presuppositions presented in Scripture:

- Marriage is to be celebrated. (John 2:1-11)

- Monogamy and permanence in marriage are valued. (Mark 10:2-9)

- Husband and wife are of equal worth before God. (Gen. 1:26-30; Ps. 139:13-16; Matt. 19:4-6; Mark 10:6-12)

- God opposes domination and/or deception in relations between sexes. (Gen. 2:18-22; Acts 2:17-18; Gal. 3:28-29; Col. 3:9-15; 1 Pet. 3:7)

The Trinity exists as one God yet three Persons. The Father, Son, and Holy Spirit have equal value but different roles. A wife and husband have equal value in God's sight but different roles. A look into the different roles must remain in the context of *love*. Love provides the security and freedom that must exist within any relationship. True love also has a way of changing a person. Scripture provides evidence of a transformational process that takes place in marriage.

Due to the work of Jesus and indwelling of the Holy Spirit, we do not need a priest or a spiritual leader to develop our personal relationship with God. We must take responsibility for our own personal, spiritual formation.

APPROACHING EPHESIANS 5

Ephesians 5 is about following Christ's example. Christ loved, gave Himself up, and sacrificed Himself (Eph. 5:1-2). Each of these characteristics requires "be[ing] kind and compassionate to one another" (Eph. 4:32). To function as one, a couple must rely on the Holy Spirit as they each member finds his or her roles.

Often the Ephesians 5 passage has been erroneously interpreted solely based on the submission of wives to their husbands. If we check our brains at the door, we might miss other challenging truths.

Every marriage settles into some type of social and organizational arrangement as both husband and wife play specific roles. There are no role-less marriages. Because the noise of our culture is so loud and confusing, few people know what roles they are functionally playing. It can be confusing to try and distinguish between true biblical roles and traditional cultural roles. Traditional cultural roles should not be seen as negative—a culture needs these constructs for structure. However, we often mistakenly attempt to adjust the Bible to support our personal mores. We should adapt to the Bible, not force the Bible to fit our lifestyles.

As you approach this passage, you'll need to understand mutual submission as stated in verse 21—"submit to one another out of reverence for Christ." *The Expositor's Bible Commentary* explains a bit more about the context of Ephesians 5: "The basic principle of Christian submissiveness that governs the community life of the church applies also to social relationships. Paul selects the most conspicuous of these and shows how they are transformed when controlled by a prior obedience to Christ."[2] After broaching the topic of Christian submission in marriage, Paul continues his discussion of Christian submission in Ephesians 6, demonstrating its application in relationships between children and parents (Eph. 6:1-4) and between slaves and masters (Eph. 6:5-9).[3] We so often focus on the call for wives to submit to husbands that we lose sight of the entirety of the passage.

Keep in mind: Paul was challenging converts to die to self as symbolized by Christ's death on the cross. Paul was in a culture war with the people of his time—he told men to use their power for the benefit of others instead of trying to gain power for themselves.

Leader, here it is important to help couples think through the purpose, beauty, and responsibility of each God-given role. While the wife is to respect and submit to her husband's leadership, she does so willingly as her husband loves her with the same kind of sacrificial love Christ showed the church. This relationship is not a picture of a domineering man barking orders at his subservient wife or a passive disengaged man withdrawing into his work or hobbies—in fact, it's quite the opposite. According to God's design, "the husband's primary responsibility as head of the household is to love, provide, protect, and serve his wife and family—not to lord [his position] over them according to his personal whims and desires."[4]

Having said all of the above, Scripture demonstrates obvious gender differences and diverse cultural approaches to living together in holy matrimony. Please keep in mind that it is okay to work through difficult passages such as Ephesians 5 together. This is one way God challenges our minds and transforms our lives.

THE ULTIMATE QUESTION

What role or function is only a wife meant to fulfill in marriage? What role or function is only a husband meant to fulfill in marriage? This is the ultimate question to ask as we study roles and responsibilities.

It is barely daybreak, and Ben is out the door for another long day at the office. Ben is an accountant at an emerging firm. Despite the demands of his job, Ben is energized because his business associates admire and respect him. He also knows that if he performs well he may soon be promoted to partner. So, he often works twelve to fourteen hours a day. He justifies it by saying, "Isn't it my job to provide for my family?"

As his wife, Jennifer, begins her day, she feels overwhelmed by the demands of her own job, not to mention paying the bills, maintaining order in their home, and running countless errands. Jennifer tries to be understanding, but rather than aiding and supporting Ben as a friend and helper, she feels distant and resentful. Ben and Jennifer have lost focus of what it means "to have and to hold." They have allowed screaming demands to replace sacred priorities.

In order "to have and to hold" for a lifetime, couples must grasp their unique, God-given roles in marriage. Ben and Jennifer were so focused on their individual tasks that they lost sight of what is important in making a marriage function.

Taking out the trash, paying the bills, cleaning the house, mowing the grass, and cooking the meals are important tasks. Thankfully, in our marriage, we have learned what each of us does better. In our home, for example, it would be challenging for Carla to handle our finances. Her idea of a balanced checkbook is anywhere within $5 to $50, but she does enjoy preparing healthy meals. Byron's night to cook means ordering pizza—unless he makes his one and only home-cooked entrée, creamed tuna on toast. For some of our friends, though, the husband is the better cook, and the wife handles the finances. So, whose job is it? We have discovered that assigning daily responsibilities becomes secondary once we understand the foundational and functional God-designed roles in marriage.

Before the wedding day, ask: 1) What is my part? and 2) How can I contribute to making order and oneness in our family so there is freedom and security as we carry out life's responsibilities?

How did working through the Bible study book go this week?

STARTER QUESTIONS FROM THE BIBLE STUDY BOOK WILL LEAD INTO THE SESSION.
In your parents' marriage, what were some of the roles that differed from biblical roles or principles? How would you like for these roles to happen in your own marriage?

In the past, what have the traditional roles of husband and wife looked like? Illustration: Look at 1950s Women's Preparation for Marriage (See p. 44.), and have some fun examining our past culture.

HELPFUL TIP: *Encourage couples to utilize their Bible study books to refer to their answers. This will provide accountability for them to continue working through their weekly assignments.*

What does today's culture say about the role of a husband and wife?

What are some roles we deem biblical but are, in fact, merely cultural?

TRANSITIONAL QUESTION: What did you learn (or what questions arose) from doing this week's assignments, especially Assignment #3, "Identify Biblical Roles and Duties"?

STATE THE PART OF THE VOWS AND PRESENT THE KEY QUESTION (P. 25) FOR THIS SECTION. PRAY.

IS THERE A DIFFERENCE BETWEEN ROLES AND RESPONSIBILITIES?

The roles of husband and wife may be a sensitive subject for some. First, let's determine if there is a difference between roles and responsibilities. Our working definition of role is a function one executes in the context of teamwork; the word does not denote privilege, rank, or status. Roles include the unique function that each person performs in the context of oneness.

Responsibilities are the daily tasks required to fulfill the functions of married life such as taking out the trash, paying bills, mowing the lawn, cooking, etc.

Let's first discuss daily responsibilities. Ask the couple(s) some fun questions regarding the day-to-day tasks of married life (responsibilities).

Do you plan to model the tasks and jobs (responsibilities) in your marriage the same way your parents did?

What similarities exist in the way you see roles within your marriage being lived out and the way your parents functioned? Differences?

Now let's talk about the expected behavior patterns a husband and a wife must fulfill to function as a team:

What issues does the Bible specifically address regarding biblical roles in marriage? What are traditional/cultural roles for each marriage partner? How are you as a couple going to determine the difference between what our culture dictates and the Bible says?

In marriage, what do you see as the husband's key role? What role or function can only a husband fulfill in marriage?

In marriage, what do you see as the wife's key role? What role or function can only a wife fulfill in marriage?

HELPFUL TIP: *Our hope is to spur conversation and discussion between the couple. Do not feel as if you have to cover all details of this section.*

WHAT CAN THE MODEL OF JESUS TEACH US?

For our discussion, we will look to Jesus Christ as our model. We have discovered that God has given husbands and wives each a distinctive primary role to fulfill in marriage. As one carries out his or her primary role, God suggests certain important responses from the other spouse in order to enable and encourage their spouse in fulfilling his or her appropriate biblical roles.

Do you desire to pattern your own life and marriage after Christ's example? Why or why not?

What words would you use to describe Jesus? Is there anything about Jesus that you would consider dishonorable? Demeaning? Disrespectful? Uncaring?

How did Christ illustrate headship? Being a helper? Submission? Praise and honor?

If Jesus perfectly modeled God's idea of both headship and submission, why does our world today often view those concepts as demeaning, disrespectful, uncaring, dishonorable, etc.?

The world's perception of Jesus' life, His perfect headship and submission, is an apt example of how our world can take what God means to be wonderful and turn it into something offensive.

Jesus is our ultimate example. The roles and responses discussed in this section are not unbecoming characteristics, causing chaos. On the contrary, they are Christlike characteristics. Though it can be challenging, we seek ways to follow in the faithful footsteps of Christ.

WHAT ARE BIBLICAL ROLES?

The Bible provides insight into the roles and responses of husband and wife. Looking to instruction from the Old and New Testaments, we simplify these into **Primary Roles** and **Important Responses** for each spouse. We must view these roles through the lens of Christ's life.

> **FOR THE HUSBAND:** *PRIMARY ROLE*—headship;
> a wife's **important response**—respect and submission

> **FOR THE WIFE:** *PRIMARY ROLE*—helper;
> a husband's **important response**—praise and honor

> *What is involved in the husband's role of headship?*

HUSBAND'S PRIMARY ROLE—HEADSHIP (EPH. 5:23; I COR. 11:2-3)

Go back and read Ephesians 5:21-23. In addition, read "A Word to Husbands" on page 42 in the synopsis of this session.

In the context of Ephesians 5 and other Scriptures, Paul uses "headship" as a metaphor to describe something that is prominent, chief, or the cornerstone.[5] *Easton's Illustrated Bible Dictionary* refers to head in this passage as "the 'house-band,' connecting and keeping together the whole family."[6]

Headship is a function of responsibility, and it fosters maturity among all family members. The goal is for the husband to cherish his wife. Headship should be like that of Christ.

> *What does headship look like? Is leadership the same as headship?*

HEADSHIP INVOLVES LEADING. (MARK 10:42-45)

Leaders typically fall into two categories: servant leaders and "lording" leaders. Obviously, when the Bible talks about headship, it does *not* refer to a lording leader. To be like Christ is to become a servant leader. It is important to understand the differences between a servant leader and a lording leader.

A lording leader:
- makes all the decisions himself;
- selfishly seeks to control others so he can meet his own needs;
- may become a passive non-leader, disengaging himself from relationships and giving little or no direction to his wife and family.

A true servant leader:
- assumes overall responsibility for the direction of his family and takes the initiative to serve the needs of his wife and family;
- works to maximize his wife's gifts and abilities;
- pours out his life on his wife's behalf so she can become all God intended;
- denies himself and gives of his life on behalf of the whole family.[7]

Is the man (husband) required to be the spiritual leader? Is it the sole responsibility of the husband to lead spiritually or can/should the wife spiritually lead too?

HEADSHIP INVOLVES LOVING. (EPH. 5:25-27)

Love is to be unconditional—just as Christ loved the church. Love is to be sacrificial—involving self-denial, placing your spouse's needs above your own. Love is to be complete—not based on performance but based on mutual acceptance. Love is commitment—based upon a determination of the will, not a passing feeling.

HEADSHIP INVOLVES CARING. (EPH. 5:28-30)

In order for a man to understand his wife's needs, he must become a student of his spouse. As a man shares life with his bride, he expresses caring by showing her she is a priority. Men must take initiative in regard to:

- Spiritual matters in the home—to pray, worship at church, and study God's Word

- Life issues—to have finances in order, ensure needs are met, and take care to make sure your wife feels secure

- Relational harmony—to forgive, resolve conflicts, and ensure your home is a place of encouragement and safety

- Decisions

- _____ (Fill in the blank—many things not listed above.)

    Do you think men today invest more energy at work than they do in maximizing the potential of their wives and children? If so, why?

A WIFE'S IMPORTANT RESPONSES TO HER HUSBAND'S ROLE OF HEADSHIP

What is the wife's response to her husband's role of headship?

Several places throughout Scripture, a wife is specifically instructed to respond to her husband's role of headship with submission and respect (Eph. 5:21-24; Col. 3:18; 1 Pet. 3:1-6).

A WIFE RESPONDS WITH SUBMISSION.

Within a husband and wife relationship, submission simply means to voluntarily organize in an orderly fashion so as to fill out a pattern that presents a complete whole.[8] This provides an effective order of accountability as we respond to God according to 1 Corinthians 11:3-8.

HOW DID CHRIST ILLUSTRATE SUBMISSION?
- Listened to and responded to God and others
- Loved and obeyed God and others
- Respected others (respectful in His behavior toward others)
- Honored God and others
- Praised God and others
- Gained strength from God

- Obeyed God's plan
- Served God and others

In response to her husband's leadership, a wife should attempt to emulate Christ.

A WIFE RESPONDS WITH RESPECT.

> "And let the wife see that she respects and reverences her husband, that she notices him, regards him, honors him, prefers him, venerates, and esteems him; and that she defers to him, praises him, and loves and admires him exceedingly."
> **EPHESIANS 5:33, AMPC**

Respect "means voluntary lifting up another person for special consideration, treatment, and obedience."[9] It has been said, "If a man is king at work and an involuntary servant at home, he will spend more time where he is admired, unchallenged, and respected."

HOW DID CHRIST SHOW RESPECT?

- Valued sinners (even prostitutes and tax collectors)
- Showed confidence in those who lacked faith
- Did not condemn
- Did not humiliate people or those who made mistakes
- Respected people

WIFE'S PRIMARY ROLE—HELPER

What is involved in the wife's role of "helper"?

The term *helper*, also used by God to identify Himself (Ex. 18:4; Deut. 33:7), describes the woman God created to partner with man in exercising dominion over the world and propagating the generations (Gen. 1:28; 2:18). There is no hint of inferiority in the term which describes function, rather than worth. As the man's "helper," the woman complements him through her own unique function in the economy of God. As one "comparable to him" (Gen. 2:18, NKJV), she, too, is created "in the image of God" (Gen. 1:27). Both man and woman fully bear God's image, but each expresses His image in unique and God-ordained ways through manhood or womanhood.

The words *help* and *meet* (or helpmate) come from *Êzer* (ay'–zer) which means "to aid; help"[10] and *neged* (neh'–ghed) meaning "a front, i.e. part opposite; specifically, a counterpart."[11] It actually comes from the root *nâgad* (naw-gad') which means "a primitive root; properly, to front, i.e. stand boldly out opposite."[12]

So when we think of a helpmeet or helper, it is one who stands boldly opposite, as a counterpart, "to front" or offer aid or assistance. The word picture which comes to mind is that of teepee poles. They serve as a counterpart to offer a strong base or foundation for the rest of the hut.

Another big picture concept to consider: being a helper involves a beneficial relationship in which one person aids or supports another as a friend and ally.

ASK THE MEN: *What are some ways you need your (future) wife's help?*

ASK THE WOMEN: *What are some ways your (future) husband needs your help?*

HELPFUL TIPS: *Create an open dialogue and establish good discussion. Allow couples to express their thoughts, opinions, and questions.*

The opposite of a helper is a competitor. Competitors do not fill in gaps or support weak areas. Instead, they exploit weaknesses to gain the upper hand. A competitive wife stirs a man to aggression, retaliation, and withdrawal rather than causing him to want to care, support, and meet her needs.

BEING A HELPER INVOLVES BEING A HOMEMAKER.

Wives need to be themselves—this is the greatest way they can help their husbands and children. A brief look at Titus 2:1-5 suggests behavior that would enhance this dynamic husband and wife relationship:

- Love your husband and children (Titus 2:4)
- Be self-controlled and pure (Titus 2:5)
- Be busy at home (Titus 2:5)

What do you think it means to be a worker at home?

God intended homemaking to be considered a privilege.

Do you think women today believe that building a career is more fulfilling than being a homemaker and rearing children? If so, why?

A HUSBAND'S IMPORTANT RESPONSES TO HIS WIFE'S BIBLICAL ROLE OF HELPER

What is the husband's response to his wife's role of helper?

Proverbs 31:28-29 and 1 Peter 3:7 encourage a husband to consistently respond to his wife with praise and honor. Although this response is often not natural for husbands, it demonstrates to our wives that we are in this journey together and we desire to maximize their full potential.

ASK MEN: *Why is your important response of praise and honor so crucial to the success of your wife's pursuit of being a helper? What might happen if she doesn't receive it from you?*

A HUSBAND RESPONDS WITH PROVISION AND PROTECTION.

In the early church, traditionally a bride would walk on the left side of her future husband. Historically, this was done so that a man could quickly to draw his sword or weapon with his right hand in order to protect his bride.

From the beginning of time, a man displays love and care for his wife and family as he works the garden (Gen. 2:15) to be used of God to provide for the basic needs of life. For men to be good husbands to their wives and live in the new life of God's grace, they should seek and find provision for their helper.

There are a multitude of ways a husband can respond to being "heirs together of the grace of life" (1 Pet. 3:7, KJV). God has designed husbands to display compassion and love to create a "unity of mind" (1 Pet. 3:8, ESV) toward their helper. Once again, the key is oneness.

WHAT IS MY PART?

Before a couple can "have and hold" one another, they must each know their part. God's Word offers encouragement to help us recognize these roles. In addition, godly friends can offer us some practical ways to get on the same page. In closing, have couples think through these useful questions:

What do you see as the most difficult adjustment your spouse will make in living with you?

What will be the biggest change for you living in with your (future) spouse?

Name a few married couples you know that are modeling healthy roles and responsibilities. What impresses you most in how they function?

Each spouse's understanding of his or her part in making a marriage team effective is a foundational asset to the marriage. As a leader facilitating this session, perhaps the most important thing you can do for these future marriages and families is to help couples follow God's principles into oneness and freedom.

Leader, remind couples that God sees them as holy and beautiful as they follow in the loving footsteps of Christ. The aforementioned roles and responses are not unbecoming characteristics but Christlike ones.

Marriage is such a privilege. Please help couples understand how valuable it is to discover God's divine instructions—and to know the part couples play in giving a righteous depiction of His kingdom to the world.

SYNOPSIS

Every marriage settles into some type of social and organizational arrangement with both husband and wife playing specific roles. There are no role-less marriages. The noise of culture has confused God's standards and values with traditional cultural roles—even in the church. True biblical principles provide structure, order, and function and will transcend time, philosophy, and ethnicity. However, we often mistakenly attempt to adjust the Bible to support our personal mores. We should adapt to the Bible, not force the Bible to fit our lifestyles. It is obvious in Scripture that there are gender differences and diverse cultural approaches to living together as one in holy matrimony.

CORE VALUES

Keep in mind, Scripture presents some core values regarding marriage:
- Marriage deemed important (John 2:1-11)
- Monogamy and permanence in marriage (Mark 10:2-9)
- Equal responsibility (Mark 10:11-12)
- God's opposition to domination and/or deception between sexes (Matt. 5:27-30)

A WORD TO HUSBANDS

In order for unity and oneness to take place, the husband must assume the God-ordained role of headship. In 1 Corinthians 11:3 and Ephesians 5:23, the Bible says the role of headship is the husband's. The word head simply means "literally or figuratively the head, cornerstone."[13] This functional role granted by God to man is not intended to be an abusive power position. Neither should men give into passivity that is driven by selfishness. Instead, as imitators of Christ, we are to look out for the best interest of all family members through love, nurture, and care. This connection fosters maturity, while nourishing and cherishing its members.

It is not easy for the head of the home to lead, love, and care for his wife; he must daily die to self—as modeled by Jesus. Please know that the benefits of this sacrificial love far outweigh the costs. As I (Byron) initiate this kind of headship for Carla, she is strengthened and nourished. This motivates her to respond positively to me as she maximizes her potential and fully becomes who God intended her to be. We both find security and freedom from the oneness this creates.

A WORD TO WIVES

In Genesis 2:18, God created woman because He decided it was not good for man to be alone. In this verse, the word *helpmeet* comes from two Hebrew words. One means "to aid or help"[14] and the other means "counterpart."[15] The root derivative of "counterpart" means "to front, i.e. part opposite."[16] Again, not a "slave" for her husband but one who boldly stands opposite to aid or help her husband become everything God desires. Wives who offer the best aid to their husbands are those who have a deep spiritual core and find their worth, value, and security in God alone. With her mighty spiritual core, the wife can be free from the need to control and manipulate as she deeply loves and serves her husband. This fosters a deeper oneness and trust.

"The Bible presents a woman as a strong image bearer of God, able to stand against the world, powerfully influencing men and culture as she lives the life God created her to live."[17]

GARY THOMAS

KIND AND COMPASSIONATE TO ONE ANOTHER

Ephesians 5 is about following Christ's example. Christ loved, gave Himself up, and sacrificed (Eph. 5:1-2). Each of these characteristics requires us to "be kind and compassionate to one another" (Eph. 4:32). To function as one, a couple must rely on God's Holy Spirit as each finds his or her role.

It is okay to work through difficult passages, such as Ephesians 5, together. This is one way God challenges our minds and transforms our lives. Keep in mind that these are radical verses from Paul to challenge men to die to self as Jesus did. Paul challenged a culture that gave men power by saying, *Use your power for the benefit of the other person.*

Before marrying one another, may God's Word challenge you first to recognize each other's value and to understand your part in making a marriage team effective. Then, you can attempt to negotiate the daily tasks of married life.

1950S WOMEN'S PREPARATION FOR MARRIAGE

The following is allegedly from a 1950s Home Economics textbook intended to teach high school girls how to prepare for married life.

1. Have dinner ready: Plan ahead, even the night before, to have a delicious meal on time. This is a way of letting [your husband] know that you have been thinking about him and are concerned about his needs. Most men are hungry when they come home, and the prospects of a good meal are part of the warm welcome needed.

2. Prepare yourself: Take 15 minutes to rest so you will be refreshed when he arrives. Touch up your makeup, put a ribbon in your hair, and be fresh looking. He has just been with a lot of work weary people. Be a little gay and a little more interesting. His boring day may need a lift.

3. Clear away the clutter: Make one last trip through the main part of the house just before your husband arrives, gathering up school books, toys, paper, etc. Then run a dust cloth over the tables. Your husband will feel he has reached a haven of rest and order, and it will give you a lift, too.

4. Prepare the children: Take a few minutes to wash the children's hands and faces (if they are small), comb their hair, and if necessary, change their clothes. They are little treasures and he would like to see them playing the part.

5. Minimize all noise: At the time of his arrival, eliminate all noise of washer, dryer, dishwasher, or vacuum. Try to encourage the children to be quiet. Be happy to see him. Greet him with a warm smile and be glad to see him.

6. Some don'ts: Don't greet him with problems or complaints. Don't complain if he's late for dinner. Count this as minor compared with what he might have gone through that day.

7. Make him comfortable: Have him lean back in a comfortable chair or suggest he lie down in the bedroom. Have a cool or warm drink ready for him. Arrange his pillow and offer to take off his shoes. Speak in a low, soft, soothing, and pleasant voice. Allow him to relax—unwind.

8. Listen to him: You may have a dozen things to tell him but the moment of his arrival is not the time. Let him talk first.

9. Make the evening his: Never complain if he does not take you out to dinner or to other places of entertainment. Instead, try to understand his world of strain and pressure, his need to be home and relax.

10. The Goal: Try to make your home a place of peace and order where your husband can renew himself in body and spirit.[18]

Take a moment to laugh and learn from our past. Think, pray, and talk through the ways you, as a couple, want to walk forward.

Are your perspectives in line with the gender role principles illustrated in the Bible?

Are the roles that you'd like to play in your marriage mutually respectful and honoring to both members of the couple?

FINANCIAL RESPONSIBILITIES

HOW MUCH IS ENOUGH?

OVERVIEW

The purpose of this section is to provide a helpful overview of financial stewardship, budgeting, and money management. In order to experience true freedom, couples must gain a balanced perspective on how to deal effectively with financial responsibilities.

"We buy things we don't need with money we don't have in order to impress people we don't like!"[1]

DAVE RAMSEY

"FOR BETTER FOR WORSE, FOR RICHER FOR POORER ..."

"God can utilize my use of His resources as a testimony to the world.
My attitude as a Christian toward wealth becomes the testimony."[2]
RON BLUE

SESSION GOAL

To help couples understand and follow God's stewardship principles as they work to experience financial freedom.

KEY BIBLICAL PRINCIPLES

- Proverbs 13:18—Self-discipline
- Proverbs 22:7—The borrower is slave to the lender.
- Ecclesiastes 5:10—Money does not satisfy.
- Malachi 3:10, Matthew 23:23, and Luke 11:42—Tithing
- Luke 12:15—Be on guard against greed.
- 1 Timothy 6:6-11,18—Flee from the love of money; share what you have.
- Hebrews 13:5-6—Be content with what you have.

*"When your outgo exceeds your income, then
your upkeep is your downfall!"[3]*
ANONYMOUS

Dear Leader,

This is one of those sections that engaged and newly married couples can pay for now or pay for later, but they must put forth the time, energy, and effort required to get on the same page regarding finances. You will need to strongly encourage couples to invest in the Prep Work this week. It will likely be one of the most time-consuming yet rewarding of the learning exercises you will have couples complete. As you know, personal finances may either bring bondage or freedom. Newly married couples chart the course of their financial future fairly early on in their marriage. Financial management skills are easy to learn. Though practical, these topics carry a large spiritual component. The Bible says, "For where your treasure is, there your heart will be also" (Matt. 6:21). We are convinced that God uses money and sex as some of the greatest life labs for spiritual formation. Money has a way of gut checking what we really believe to be true about life. Pray for God to use each of this week's couple interactions to teach them much about themselves and their faithful God.

Early in our marriage, Carla was forced to take me more for the "worse and the poorer" than the "better and the richer." When my dad had to wire us money on our honeymoon, the reality of this part of the marriage vows hit us very quickly.

I often joke that it took two weeks of marriage to deplete twenty-one years of savings. As my dad reminded me, "Looks like you didn't save enough over the twenty-one years." This is a constant struggle for all of us—we spend more than we save. My dad used to tell me, "Son, it doesn't matter if you make $300 or $30,000 per month; you must discipline yourself to spend less than you make."

You may need self-discipline more in this area than in any other area covered in this study (except maybe sex). Perhaps this is why money management plays such a big part in character development. Thankfully, Scripture is full of encouragement as to how to deal with money.

> "Where your treasure is, there will your heart be also."
> **MATTHEW 6:21, KJV**

Despite the multitude of money management resources, it seems Americans aren't getting the message. The 2016 American Household Credit Card Debt Study found that most U.S. households have an average of $134,643 in debt, including mortgages.[4] The majority of Americans live from paycheck to paycheck.[5] We have not learned the self-discipline concepts of delayed gratification and spending less than we earn.

In the first five years of marriage, a couple can either build a foundation that leads to financial freedom or bury themselves in debt and bondage that will force them to dig out over the next ten to fifteen years. After more than twenty years of working with young couples, we have observed the patterns established in those crucial first five years are determined through the behaviors of the first eighteen months of marriage.

Unless you learn and apply these financial management concepts early on, more than likely, you will experience stress in your marriage. In fact, financial difficulty (lack of compatibility in how spouses handle finances—one prefers to spend while another values saving) is one of the main reasons cited for divorce.[6]

It is important to discuss the following areas of personal finances with your partner:
- When to combine bank accounts and titles to vehicles or homes
- Planning and living on a budget
- The primary caretaker for paying bills and balancing the checkbook
- Career plans
- Long-term financial planning including life insurance and making a will
- Saving and investments

As you continue to discover and experience the best that married life has to offer, it is important to gain a balanced perspective as to how to deal effectively with financial responsibilities. Heads up, this section may be time-consuming, but it will save you time, energy, and money in the future. It will require some hard work and honesty. Keep in mind, money has a way of gut checking what we really believe to be true.

How did working through the Bible study book go this week?

STARTER QUESTIONS FROM THE BIBLE STUDY BOOK WILL LEAD INTO THE SESSION.

Did you fight while working through the budget? (Ask humorously, but be sensitive to couples who might have struggled. Remind them that it is common for couples to have disagreements and arguments over money.)

How did your budgeting discussions go?

Are you a saver or a spender? What do you expect from your (future) spouse?

What happens if your money runs out before your expenses do?

As a couple, did you come up with ways to save money? Do you have a financial plan (or goals) for your marriage?

TRANSITIONAL QUESTION: What challenges do you think you will face as a couple going from my money to our money?

STATE THE PART OF THE VOWS AND PRESENT THE KEY QUESTION (P. 47) FOR THIS SECTION.

PRAY.

```
┌─────────────────────────────────┐
│     DRIVING QUESTION            │
│       (40 minutes)              │
└─────────────────────────────────┘
```

WHAT ARE YOUR CONCERNS ABOUT FINANCES?

As you transition couples to consider the Driving Questions, check the pulse of the couples by asking if they have anxieties concerning money.

What are some of your common frustrations concerning money matters?

Does money stress you out? Does money control you? What are your biggest concerns with the way your (future) spouse handles finances?

Do you have concerns about your debt? Your partner's debt?

Why do you think money is one of the major causes for divorce in our country?

Should both husband and wife work outside of the home? What about if children enter the family?

Where money is concerned, our future intentions shape our immediate plans.

NOTE: *If a couple desires for a parent to stay home and raise the children, it's wise to learn to live off of one income and save or invest the rest.*

There are several keys to financial freedom.

- Remember, God owns it all!

- Money is never an end in and of itself. It is merely a resource used to accomplish other goals and obligations.

- There will always be a trade-off between time and effort, money and rewards.

- If we spend less than we earn and do it for a long time, we will be financially successful.

- Delayed gratification is crucial!

LET'S TALK BUDGETING.

Using the budget suggestions in the Bible study book and reviewing their financial situation, couples will have the necessary tools to establish a budget and to guard against problem areas that might become budget busters. No budget will implement itself. Couples must put forth effort and prioritize family communication. Living on a budget is not only practical, but it is absolutely necessary in order to maintain a debt-free lifestyle.

Who handled the money in your family growing up? Mom? Dad? Both? Neither? Who will be primarily responsible for the finances in your new family?

Is shopping a privilege, right, or chore?

HELPFUL TIP: *Establish a working budget and evaluate it often. Set financial goals, and learn to control monthly cash flow. Keep your method simple.*

ESTABLISH A WORKING BUDGET.

Practice the 10-70-20 plan. After you tithe 10 percent and pay your taxes, use 100 percent of your net spendable income in the following way:

- *10%*   *Savings—pay yourself (retirement)*
- *70%*   *Living expenses*
- *20%*   *Debt and/or future planning*

We commend to you this excellent biblical principle in Proverbs 13:11, "Whoever gathers money little by little makes it grow." Here are some practical steps to encourage couples to gather little by little.

- *Step 1: Establish a $1,000 emergency fund.*
- *Step 2: Begin to pay off consumer debt and work toward saving two or three months worth of living expenses for unanticipated situations.*
- *Step 3: Begin short-term savings for future planning (auto, appliances, furniture, etc.).*
- *Step 4: Generate long-term savings for things like a house down payment or your kids' college funds.*

Many couples begin marriage significantly in debt. These statistics might be helpful, comforting, or motivating to help couples concentrate on getting rid of their debt.

Remind couples that it takes less energy to earn a living than to earn a living and pay back debts.

Have couples analyze their budget on page 106 of the Bible study book and compare it with the "Budget Thoughts: Ways to Avoid Potential Problems— Identifying Red Flags" handout.
(See The Tools, p.62 and online at LifeWay.com/ToHaveAndToHold.)

NOTE: *A tool on crown.org allows couples to plug in income and expenses to analyze their budget situation.*

HAVE YOU DISCUSSED DEBT?

When (if ever) do you borrow?

Debt presumes on the future and may deny God an opportunity to work. How do you plan to move forward concerning debt?

How do you get out of debt?

To help couples get out of debt, we suggest they:

- *Establish a workable budget.*
- *Determine ways to increase their cash flow margin.*
- *Begin to pay off consumer debt starting with highest interest rate first.*
- *After they've paid off the debt with the highest interest rate, they should apply those payments and add the minimum payment amount for the second debt (the debt with the second highest interest rate).*

WHAT DOES THE BIBLE SAY ABOUT MONEY?

Money is mentioned often in the Bible. It is vital to life and crucial to provision for a family. No one should ever apologize about being compensated for his or her hard work. Yet, life and work balance must not be driven by a desire for more possessions. Money does not bring contentment. You must keep a right financial perspective in marriage.

Have someone read the following texts aloud and sum them up with one phrase.

- *Ecclesiastes 5:10—Money does not satisfy.*
- *Mark 10:17-31—Be careful that money doesn't become an idol and blind you from God's kingdom purposes.*
- *1 Timothy 6:6-11,18—Flee from the love of money; share what you have.*

CHRIST TAUGHT ABOUT FINANCES.

Christ never said money or material things were problems. But, He said the love of money can be the root of all kinds of problems.

Read Luke 12:15-21. What did Jesus identify as more important than material possessions?

It surprises many Christians to learn that approximately two-thirds of the parables that Christ used in His teaching deal specifically with finances, the things we own, and how we utilize the resources God has given us.[7]

Christ constantly warned us to guard our hearts against greed, covetousness, ego, and pride because these are some of the tools that Satan uses to control and manipulate this world.

> "He said to them, 'Beware, and be on your guard against
> every form of greed; for not even when one has an
> abundance does his life consist of his possessions.'"
> **LUKE 12:15, NASB**

GOD OWNS IT ALL!

Everyone comes into the world with nothing and leaves with nothing. All riches were here before we arrived, and they will be here when we depart. "'The silver is mine, and the gold is mine,' declares the LORD Almighty" (Hag. 2:8). During our life on earth, we are each entrusted with certain gifts, talents, and opportunities. What are you going to do with the resources available to you? How will you spend His money that He's given you to steward? God tells us to give freely to His work through our tithe. But we shouldn't stop there, our lives should be about helping others.

DO YOU TRUST GOD TO BE YOUR PROVIDER?

Faith, according to Hebrews 11, is trusting God completely. It means trusting God for the things we cannot see or manipulate into happening. Most of us truly desire to be able to exercise this kind of faith, but the world around us tells us to do just the opposite. If we do not have the money for what we "need," then we borrow to buy it. If we want something too expensive for our income, so what? The world says we deserve it, so go for it!

God's Word tells us to learn to be content and dedicate ourselves to serving God.

> "Let us also lay aside every encumbrance and the
> sin which so easily entangles us, and let us run with
> endurance the race that is set before us."
> **HEBREWS 12:1, NASB**

BEING RICH

Rich is a subjective term used, in context, to describe having enough money to meet all of our reasonable needs with funds left over. Clearly, God's Word teaches that many of His people will fit into this category. God's plan is clearly stated in 2 Corinthians 8:14-15. Our abundance at the present time will meet the needs of others, and later, their abundance will meet our needs. If you have an abundance, it is your responsibility to help others!
Christ warned those who are rich to always be on their guard (Luke 12:15-21). It's very tempting to trust in the security that a surplus may provide. The greater the surplus, the greater the temptation. That's why those who are rich (most of American Christianity) must guard their hearts and minds with principles from God's Word.

Do not plan God out of your finances. He wants to complete a good work in you—*trust Him*. He knows what He is doing. Do your part by *obeying*.

A faith plan involves:
1. Not always being able to see how the goal is going to be accomplished
2. Having inadequate resources to accomplish the objective
3. Not knowing what the next step to fulfill God's plan will be
4. Knowing that God is always faithful

In what specific ways do you trust our faithful God to provide for you?

What do you know or what have you learned regarding stewardship?

What are your financial goals for the present? In one to three years? Twenty years? Forty years?

FINANCIAL GOALS

To reach worthy financial or life goals, a person will have to practice a lifestyle of self-discipline and deny self many of the treasures of this world. A couple will have to compromise and agree on financial priorities for their family and then stick to those commitments. It is important for parents to teach these principles to their children and prepare them for disciplined living.

As you conclude, give couples a copy of "Ten Things You Can Do to Find Financial Freedom." (See The Tools, p.64.) Ask them to review the article and determine two to three practical ways they can begin to discover financial freedom. Encourage couples to bring this document out about every six months and assess how they are doing.

The first five years of marriage build a financial foundation. Challenge couples to:

- Establish healthy patterns the first eighteen months of their marriage

- Attend a money management seminar, such as Dave Ramsey's Financial Peace University or Crown Financial Resources, during the first year of marriage.

- List four or five financial goals to work toward as a couple.

- Consistently re-evaluate their overall financial situation by coming back to the financial section in their Bible study books in the weeks and years to come.

As marriage educators, our job is to help couples get off to a great start in financial freedom by understanding and following God's stewardship principles. Throughout history, these biblical principles have proven to be some of the most sound financial principles. In Christian marriages, we have an opportunity to live differently. What a blessing to be married!

SYNOPSIS

WE NEED HELP.

The first step to financial freedom is to acknowledge that your loving, sovereign God owns it all. Money has a unique way of asking, "What do you believe about God?" and then showing your answer by the way you live.

Jesus seemed to believe that the way a person manages financial resources is an outward indicator of important character traits. In Matthew 6:21, Jesus said "For where your treasure is, there your heart will be also." Every person has the privilege of managing the resources God has entrusted to him or her.

At several points in our marriage, we have been challenged by circumstances that caused us to see whether we really believed God owns all and controls all. When our two-year-old son battled cancer, God used His people, the church, to meet every need we faced. From meals to massive medical bills, our church family acknowledged that God owns and controls everything. God's people responded in obedience to His prompting and helped provide for our financial needs.

After two years of chemotherapy, radiation, surgery, more than one hundred hospital stays, and countless doctor's appointments, we concluded our experience without owing one penny. It was truly miraculous considering our meager youth ministry salary. Realistically, we could not have paid a fraction of the cost out of our own resources, yet God provided and His people obeyed. We learned a valuable lesson about God's provision—up close and personal. We also learned the equally important visual lesson in obedience.

REAL PERSPECTIVE

Our heavenly Father provides guiding principles for us so that we might be trusted to care for all of His creation. With the transfer of wealth comes responsibility. Hopefully this motivates you to understand stewardship, budgeting, money management, and how to deal effectively with financial matters.

It has been said that how one spends his or her time and money reveals true character. God can use our finances to mold us into His image, complete with self-control, patience, faithfulness, and honesty.

FINANCIAL FREEDOM

Remember, God owns it all! Money is never an end in and of itself but merely a resource used to accomplish other goals and obligations. There is always a trade-off between time and effort, money and rewards. If we spend less than we earn and do so for a long time, we will be financially successful. Delayed gratification is the key.

Money is one of the resources God uses to accomplish the real goals and objectives of life. As you struggle with your budget, overspending, and major spending decisions, rest assured that all of these struggles are spiritual development tools. Money can form you into the image of God, or it can deform you with worry, stress, and out-of-control living. The challenge is not to plan God out of your finances. He wants to complete a good work in you. Trust Him. He knows what He is doing. We must do our part—obey!

My dad may not have been surprised by my honeymoon plea from Mexico. But, through it all, learning how to manage our finances has helped Carla and me become more responsible individuals, fully committed to one another for better for worse, for richer for poorer.

THE TOOLS

BUDGET THOUGHTS: WAYS TO AVOID POTENTIAL PROBLEMS—IDENTIFYING RED FLAGS

HOUSING

Housing often proves to be problem area in budgeting. When buying or renting, stop to make sure you are making choices that fall within your budget. Your total housing expenses (mortgage, taxes, insurance, utilities, phone, and maintenance) should average below thirty-eight percent of your net spendable income. Don't take out a second mortgage for a down payment or finance your closing costs.

FOOD

When purchasing food for your family, the goal is to buy just enough. Meal planning, including a static shopping list, can really help you purchase what you need and no more. Plan trips to the grocery store when you're not hungry and not rushed. Try to avoid grocery shopping with young children. Keep an eye out for miscellaneous items, such as paper products and cleaning supplies, at bulk and discount stores. Be willing to try generic brands and plan your menu according to weekly specials.

AUTOMOBILE—PURCHASE AND MAINTENANCE

When it comes to cars, ask yourself: Do I really need a new car? Would it be possible to fix up my current vehicle or purchase a well-maintained use car? Do not lease vehicles. Be mindful of maintenance costs. When possible, perform your own repairs and maintenance. Work to ensure that auto costs (monthly payment, repairs and maintenance, gas and oil, tags and taxes, and insurance) are below fifteen percent of your net spendable income.

DEBTS

Work to minimize your debt payments (credit cards, bank loans including home equity loans, and installment credit) to below five percent of your net spendable income. Avoid credit card debt. Set a plan to pay off each credit card and creditor monthly. Be willing to sacrifice desires until you are current with your payments.

INSURANCE

Use a well-informed and trusted insurance agent to determine the best possible provision for the money. Consider buying term life insurance. If medical insurance is not part of your employment package, research major medical insurance.

RECREATION/ENTERTAINMENT

When planning recreation or entertainment, book flights and hotels as early as possible. Consider vacation locales within driving distance to avoid costly airfare. Work to vacation in the off season. Brainstorm creative and low-cost entertainment options like game night or enjoying local state parks.

CLOTHING

Save money specifically for a clothing fund. Forecast your clothing needs: buying on clearance or consignment and purchasing versatile clothing staples.

MEDICAL AND DENTAL

Medical and dental expenses are an inevitable part of life. Plan accordingly. Work to integrate healthy eating, consistent exercise, and rest into your daily life, along with appropriate hygiene habits. Prioritize preventative care and communicate with your health care providers regarding treatment and cost plans before you receive the treatment. Don't be afraid to research generic prescriptions and look for deals.

SAVINGS

Prioritize saving in your budget. Families should not plan to borrow or accrue debt consistently. When we plan to live off of credit, we're not planning for financial health. Save for both short-term purchases, such as electronics, appliances, and cars, and long-term purchases, such as a down payment on a home. Take advantage of payroll deduction, if it's available, to put a portion of your take home pay immediately in savings. You may also use a banking feature called automatic withdrawal to help you set aside some money each month.[8]

TEN THINGS YOU CAN DO TO FIND FINANCIAL FREEDOM

1. **PRAY DAILY.** The foundation of financial freedom is spiritual. God provides for you and He wants you to use His resources in a way that brings Him glory. Foster an attitude of gratitude. Pray about your financial choices. Ask God to help you see and steward your money rightly. "In everything give thanks; for this is God's will for you in Christ Jesus" (1 Thess. 5:18, NASB).

2. **CHECK YOUR PAYCHECK.** This goes without saying—spend less than you're bringing home each month. Of course, unforeseen emergencies pop up, but you will quickly lose your financial health if you *plan* to spend more money than you have in the bank. "I spoke to you in your prosperity; but you said, 'I will not listen!' This has been your practice from your youth, that you have not obeyed My voice" (Jer. 22:21, NASB).

3. **BUDGET FOR THE BEST.** Develop a monthly budget and let it guide your daily spending. Are you consistently without enough money to cover your expenses at the end of the month? Sit down and evaluate where you can cut back to make ends meet. "Commit your works to the Lord, and your plans will be established" (Prov. 16:3, NASB).

4. **BE GENEROUS.** God is pleased by generosity and giving because they show Him that we trust His provision in the coming days. We know that He provides for our needs and we want to use the money He's given us to help those around us who may have a need. In addition to blessing others and honoring God, generosity spurs us on toward sanctification in the area of finance. We want to make sure that the love of money doesn't take root in our hearts. "Be rich in good works ... be generous and ready to share" (1 Tim. 6:18, NASB).

5. **CUT THE CREDIT.** Don't be afraid to cut up any credit cards that you cannot pay off each month. Plan your big purchases ahead of time and save up for them so you won't have to buy them on credit. Evaluate your current debt and refuse to go any further into debt. "The rich rules over the poor, and the borrower becomes the lender's slave" (Prov. 22:7, NASB).

6. **CULINARY HELPS.** Who doesn't love a night on the town? Occasional dinners out are tasty and fun. But, they can pack a wallop to the wallet. Plan your budget to include a few dinners out each month. But, learn to prioritize meals at home. Make meal prep a family affair. Cooking together is a great

time to check in with one another and discuss the occurrences of the day. Then, you will have quality time as a couple and delicious meal to boot. "Poverty and shame will come to him who neglects discipline, but he who regards reproof will be honored" (Prov. 13:18, NASB).

7. **ROAD TRIP.** Before you book the Caribbean cruise, take this opportunity to explore the hidden gems that may be in your neighboring states. Grand vacations can be quite costly and are easily forgotten. Go local. "The mind of man plans his way, but the Lord directs his steps" (Prov. 16:9, NASB).

8. **LIFESTYLES OF THE RICH AND FAMOUS.** We are constantly bombarded by images and stories of others taking exotic vacations, purchasing luxury cars and homes, and buying designer clothing. Social media, shrewd marketing schemes, and our desire for nice things all seem to tell us that we *must* have the next new thing. Or, everyone else has this new item, and we have to keep up. As a Christian, you will be called to live counter-culturally in many ways. Finances are part of that dying to self. Be careful not to envy or compare your life with that of others. Bring your needs and budget before the Lord in prayer. Think about your long-term financial goals. Is it more important to have the next new thing? Or to save toward a family home in years to come? "Every labor and every skill which is done is the result of rivalry between a man and his neighbor. This too is vanity and striving after wind" (Eccl. 4:4, NASB).

9. **LOVE THE ONE YOU'RE WITH.** The car you're with, that is. Maintenance for an older car is much cheaper than the payments you'll incur when you purchase a new auto. Many people will purchase a car on credit because they don't have the cash flow to pay for repairs on their current car. In the end, new car purchases can significantly derail your budget plan. Proceed with caution. "Which one of you, when he wants to build a tower, does not first sit down and calculate the cost to see if he has enough to complete it?" (Luke 14:28, NASB).

10. **NEED OR WANT?** We live in an instant gratification world. To become financially free, we may have to discipline ourselves to say no to things now so that we can be fiscally successful down the road. Before you make a purchase, ask yourself: Do I really need this? Will I use this in the long-term?[9]

Visit LifeWay.com/ToHaveAndToHold for more financial resources and planning helps.

EMOTIONAL INTIMACY

HOW DO WE MAINTAIN A CONNECTION?

OVERVIEW

The purpose of this section is to challenge your thinking regarding emotional needs, intimacy, and oneness in marriage. We want to help you establish a strong commitment in marriage that lovingly fulfills these emotional needs. Love is based on a commitment of the will, not a passing feeling.

> *"Deep emotional intimacy is when we feel wholly accepted, respected, and admired in the eyes of our mate even when they know our innermost struggles and failures."* [1]
>
> **JILL SAVAGE**

> # "IN SICKNESS AND IN HEALTH, TO LOVE, HONOR, AND CHERISH, TILL DEATH DO US PART."

"A good marriage isn't something you
find, it's something you make."[2]
GARY THOMAS

SESSION GOAL

To challenge the couple's thinking regarding needs, intimacy, and oneness in marriage. Also to provide insight into the meaning of committed love that sustains a satisfying marriage through many years.

KEY BIBLICAL PRINCIPLES

- Genesis 2:18,22-25—Companionship and oneness defined
- Romans 15:7—Acceptance of one another
- 1 Corinthians 13—Love defined
- Ephesians 5:25-33—Love and sacrifice as Christ loved
- Philippians 2:3-5—Unselfishness; consider others as more important than self

"He is altogether lovely. This is my beloved, and this is my friend ..."
SONG OF SOLOMON 5:16, KJV

Dear Leader,

Heads up! This session may be difficult to lead, primarily because most young couples are still enamoured with one another. Since your couple(s) are in the honeymoon stage, challenge them to look down the road as they establish healthy patterns that help them connect. Challenge their current perceptions and realities, but keep them focused on the positivity of marital oneness. As a leader, you have the knowledge and insight to realize that marital satisfaction is directly related to a strong, committed love. Help couples realize what that looks like.

Enjoy the process. This is a much needed session. It may not pay dividends for years, but couples need to know they are okay and going to make it even when that heightened romantic feelings end. When romantic love ebbs, a deeper connection takes place. The blessing of marriage is experiencing true intimacy.

When Byron and I were engaged, we would go to dinner and see married couples sitting in silence. Sometimes the husband would be reading the newspaper. We would stand in judgment, wondering how they could let their marriage become so b-o-r-i-n-g. We knew *that* would never happen to *us*. We believed that our relationship would always be fueled by the intense romantic feelings we felt during our engagement, and conversation would always flow easily. Now, after years of marriage, we are not so quick to judge. As a matter of fact, we have found ourselves at restaurants struggling to find something to talk about besides our children. The temptation to pull out the newspaper is real. Or better yet, the temptation to both become captivated by the screens of our electronic devices.

Needless to say, we have realized in our own marriage that intimacy and romance do not just happen. Intimacy requires a commitment to love each other in spite of the disappointments and difficulties we face. The marriage vows "in sickness and in health, to love, honor, and cherish, till death do us part" promises a lifelong commitment.

How will you keep your marriage exciting and deepen your love for your mate in years to come? This is one of the important questions for you to address as you begin a new marriage.

In many relationships, once the honeymoon is over, the marriage slowly becomes lukewarm. Each spouse gradually begins to take the other for granted. Days turn into months, and months turn into years. For many couples, what began as a close and intimate relationship disintegrates. Often two people are simply living under the same roof—sharing a bed, bathroom, and closet—physically in the same home, yet miles apart emotionally.

Don't allow that to be a part of your story. Work to prioritize your relationship with your spouse. Ask good questions and listen intently. Pray for your spouse consistently and ask God to help you understand how to best serve him or her emotionally.

PREP WORK
(10 minutes)

How did working through the Bible study book go this week?

STARTER QUESTIONS FROM THE BIBLE STUDY BOOK WILL LEAD INTO THE SESSION.

What creative and out of the ordinary did you do for your (future) spouse this week?

How would you define intimacy? Does your definition look different from your (future) spouse's?

HELPFUL TIP: *Remember to be creative—use your own personal examples and allow time for couple interaction.*

TRANSITIONAL QUESTION: Did you take the Five Love Languages test? What is your primary love language?

STATE THE PART OF THE VOWS AND PRESENT THE KEY QUESTION (P. 67) FOR THIS SECTION.

PRAY.

CAN YOU LIVE WITH THEM? CAN THEY LIVE WITH YOU?

Socrates said "To know thyself is the beginning of wisdom."[3] At this point, most of the individuals you are working with know themselves or at least have some idea of who they are. However, it is entirely different to fully know their mates.

We all have expectations coming into marriage. Some of the expectations we have for our partners may be unrealistic simply because they don't match "what we want!"

Begin discussing the Driving Questions on emotional intimacy by first asking some questions to help couples better understand one another.

Name two or three of your "good" habits. Name two or three of your "annoying" habits. How do you feel about your partner's habits?

Do you respect and accept each other's habits and baggage? If not, why is it so difficult for you? Is there a particular issue that trips you up?

How much "me time" do you need? Do you think your partner will respect and allow your "me time"?

Illustration: Two Rowboats (See The Tools, p.83.)

What creates the most stress in your life? What causes the greatest frustration in your life? How have you seen your (future) spouse handle stress, frustration, and anger? Is this a response you can live with? Why or why not? If you are blessed with children, would you want them to follow this model?

Picture a gardener. When someone plants a garden, he or she is the thrilled to see the seed come out of the ground. The garden is beautiful as it grows. The gardener appreciates and enjoys it for a season, but inevitably weeds and other destructive forces begin to take their toll on the flowers and the foods. Does the gardener sit back and watch this destruction happen and simply wish for it to die? Absolutely not. So it is with our hope to keep marriage exciting. Like a gardener, you and your partner must work to improve and protect your relationship—shielding it from threats (without and within) while nourishing the relationship and pulling out the weeds that come in everyday life.

THE CHALLENGE OF INTIMACY

According to marriage and family expert Dr. James Dobson, twelve things commonly undermine a marriage:

- *Overcommitment and physical exhaustion*
- *Excessive credit and conflict over how money will be spent*
- *Selfishness—givers and takers*
- *Interference from in-laws*
- *Unrealistic expectations*
- *Space invaders—violating the breathing room needed by a partner*
- *Sexual frustration*
- *Business failure*
- *Business success*
- *Getting married too young*
- *Alcohol or substance abuse*
- *Pornography, gambling, and other addiction[4]*

Often couples share everyday life together—living in the same house, going through the routine of raising children, preparing meals, and commuting to work—and never take the time to connect emotionally. This type of selfishness, even when unintentionally done, destroys intimacy and may result in isolation. In strong, intimate marriages, spouses take time out to listen to one another. An emotionally intimate marriage will require commitment, hard work, and intentionality.

Name some of the ways you plan to deepen your relationship with your spouse in the years to come.

CAN YOU BE VULNERABLE?

Deepening a marital relationship requires vulnerability. Being "naked and not ashamed" is much more than just physical. In fact, the definition of intimacy—or "into-me-see"[5]—describes an openness and full disclosure that God designed for relationships. For an open, honest, and transparent bond in marriage it is necessary to create emotional safety in marriage.

GOD'S PLAN FOR INTIMACY

In Genesis 2:18-25 God saw that it was not good for man to be alone. Even though Adam had a perfect environment, perfect position, and a perfect relationship with God, he was alone. God's solution to Adam's dilemma was to create Eve to be a companion for Adam. They were to be naked and not ashamed. In God's plan, He designed marriage to be characterized by closeness, companionship, and oneness.

According to *The Pursuit of Intimacy*, each of us has genuine God-given needs for intimacy. We were created for relationships with God and with others.[6] Things cannot satisfy our emotional and spiritual needs. Intimacy needs can only be met by emotional and spiritual commodities administered through emotional and spiritual beings. It's not a sign of weakness to admit we have needs. However, in God's sovereign plan, He created us with needs so we might lovingly relate to Him and to one another, looking beyond ourselves for the supply.

This week in the Prep Work, couples discussed their Top Ten Commonly Identified Intimacy Needs (Bible study book, Assignment #4). Have couples share what they learned from one another during this assignment.

What did you learn about meeting each other's needs from Prep Work Assignment #4?

What is the easiest emotion for you to experience? What is the most difficult?

What makes it easier for you to be open and vulnerable? What makes it difficult?

Can your partner be vulnerable? Why or why not?

If vulnerability doesn't happen during dating or courtship or engagement, then how do you think it will be different in marriage?

With what part of giving of yourself do you struggle the most?

We fail to honor and cherish one another for a multitude of reasons. We often drift toward loneliness as a result.

We all want to be loved. Oftentimes, the things that matter to women just don't matter that much to men. And vice versa. Men and women have very different needs in a marriage. Generally, men feel more loved when they feel honored. Women resonate more with being cherished.

TO HONOR

Merriam-Webster's dictionary defines *honor* as "respect that is given to someone who is admired; good reputation—good quality or character as judged by other people;[7] a good name; public esteem; a showing of merited respect; a person of superior standing."[8]

Social science researcher Shaunti Feldhahn has conducted four or five longitudinal surveys of more than fourteen thousand people. More specifically, Feldhahn coordinated one survey of men and one survey of women only. Separately, Feldhahn's team studied a randomly selected national sample of four hundred heterosexual men and women ages twenty-one to seventy-five who lived within the U.S.[9]

In one of Feldhahn's studies, three out of four men said that if they had to make a choice they would give up feeling that their wives loved them if they could feel like their wives respected and valued them. Men want to feel like their wives believe in them—value, trust, admire, and appreciate them.[10]

Women often don't realize how easily they might be questioning their man's integrity or standing in life. For example: Questioning a husband's decisions all the time might be a way of criticizing him. Indirectly telling him what to do might be interpreted as questioning the husband's standing in the relationship and telling him that he is not admired.

Women are hurting men and not even realizing it.

How can a wife positively show honor to her husband?

When husbands feel inadequate or like they are not admired, they may back off becoming passive, withdrawing, or growing angry. The wife may say, "I wish he was more engaged." However, the wife may have unwittingly contributed to the husband's lack of engagement. Wives don't realize how much they inadvertently shut their husbands down.

Women, expressing appreciation for the little and big things men do can help men feel loved and honored.

TO CHERISH

In his book, *Cherish: The One Word That Changes Everything for Your Marriage*, Gary Thomas differentiates the verbs "to love" and "to cherish" by using ballet as an example. He writes, "A ballerina has to be strong, athletic, and have endurance. The moves are physically demanding. But that's similar to an NFL linebacker, who also must be strong, athletic, and have endurance. What sets the ballerina apart is the grace, the beauty, the poetry. Love is the athletic strength of marriage— unquestionably the supporting spiritual mechanism of any union. Cherish is the grace, the poetry, and the beauty of enjoyment. It takes your marriage to another place and makes it not only beautiful to dance, but beautiful to watch."[11]

In her research of four hundred women across the U.S., Shaunti Feldhahn asked women the question, "How beneficial is it to you when your husband/significant other tells you that he finds you beautiful?" Almost ninety percent of the women said it makes them feel good or made their day.[12]

More than likely, the men in your group will stare blankly when you ask them to define the word *cherish*. Yet, that word will resonate quickly with the women. Encourage women to coach their (future) husbands in a better understanding of how to cherish them.

Women, describe some ways your (future) spouse can cherish you.

"To cherish" your (future) wife is to go out of your way to make her feel she is the most beautiful person on the planet. It's a way to make her feel special and to help her know that you notice her.

ARE YOU WILLING TO LOVE EACH OTHER SACRIFICIALLY AND UNCONDITIONALLY?

Make a commitment to love each other sacrificially and unconditionally. Love is a commitment of the will, not a passing feeling or a storm of emotion. Love's source is found in God's love for us (1 John 4:7,19).

"No love of the natural heart is safe unless the human heart has been satisfied by God first."[13]

OSWALD CHAMBERS

To really love our spouses, we must accept them completely just as they are (Rom. 15:7). Trying to change them will destroy intimacy. We can only change ourselves.

In what ways has your partner demonstrated unconditional love?

How would you define love? How does this definition compare with what you thought love was in the past?

Committed love also requires sacrifice. To have an intimate marriage, we are called to give day to day to our spouse. The word *sacrifice* is defined as "the forfeiture of something highly valued for the sake of someone or something considered as having a greater value."[14]

What are some things (tangible or intangible) you have forfeited or given up for the sake of your (future) spouse?

Investing deposits of time, conversation, touch, humor, friendship, recreation, and praying together requires each of us giving up our own agendas and selfish desires for the benefit of our spouses.

HELPFUL TIP: *Be sure to give examples from your own marriage.*

EMOTIONAL BANK ACCOUNT

The best practical illustration when trying to manage emotional intimacy within marriage is to think in terms of a bank account (sometimes called an Emotional Bank, Emotional Tank, Love Bank, etc.). Each spouse has an Emotional Bank. Every contact with one's spouse, verbal or non-verbal, is either a deposit or a withdrawal.[15]

For example, suppose you've have had a tough day. You send your spouse a signal. You slam the door when you get home, let out frustration, and drop your stuff loudly on the table. This a withdrawal from your spouse's Emotional Bank.

Let's say the next morning you realize what a jerk you have been. You bring your spouse coffee in bed and say, "I'm sorry I was so frustrated last night. Will you forgive me?" Deposit!

Suppose your spouse has a tough day at work. An employee has stretched his or her patience to the limit. Your spouse starts to tell you about it after dinner. You are tired from the day and fold your arms as you stare out the window—big time withdrawal from the Emotional Bank.

No idea is more practical for marriage than understanding the principle of Emotional Bank Accounts. Couples make deposits of time, conversation, touch, humor, friendship, recreation, praying together, and unconditional love.

In a marriage that is not fulfilling and satisfying, most of the draining problems would go away if couples would apply the concept of the Emotional Bank Account every day.

Your spouse needs emotional love. He or she is going to "bank" somewhere. He or she has to—that's the way we are wired.

Encourage couples to learn their spouse's account number and make sure deposits exceed withdrawals ten to one. Remember, it is easier to withdraw than to deposit. Deposits require time and usually sacrifice.

Jesus is the ultimate model of unconditional and sacrificial love. List five descriptive words that characterize Jesus' life and might offer guidance to your relationship.

HOW DO YOU PLAN TO KEEP THE ROMANCE GOING AFTER MARRIAGE?

Do you feel more emotionally connected now than you did early in your relationship? If yes, how? If no, what can you do to nurture that emotional intimacy?

When someone close to you is sick, how do you currently respond? When you are sick, how do you want your spouse to respond?

WAYS TO MAINTAIN INTIMACY

Mutually give to meet each other's needs. Since our needs are such powerful motivators of our behavior, it is important to strongly emphasize to the couples the danger of becoming selfish and demanding, trying to take from each other rather than mutually giving and serving one another. It is also important to remind couples to look to God ultimately for their needs, to remember that He is the true source of supply (Phil. 4:19).

Illustration: "Unhealthy vs. Healthy Relationships" (See The Tools, p.84.) If possible, share a personal story.

Many times young couples, especially wives, think their new spouses should automatically know their needs—only to realize time and time again their spouses are completely clueless!

REMEMBER WHAT IS MOST IMPORTANT.

Maintain a clear perspective of what is most important in life. Remember to deposit more energy in "the bank" than you expend. Close with personal and inspirational illustrations that reiterate three points:

- *Giving to meet your spouse's needs*
- *Loving sacrificially*
- *Remembering what is most important*

This session may be tough to lead because couples are so often crazy in love at this stage of their relationship. We need to help motivate them to forecast twelve to fifteen years down the road and begin to short-circuit negative patterns that have a way of slowing and eroding emotional intimacy.

As you design this session, challenge the couples' perceptions and realities regarding marital oneness by providing insight into the meaning of a committed love. Committed love ultimately produces marital satisfaction and longevity.

A satisfying marriage is a sacred gift. Cherish it.

"Things which matter most must never be at the mercy of things which matter least."[16]

JOHANN WOLFGANG VON GOETHE

SYNOPSIS

As a married couple, the norm is to share a bedroom, bank account, and kids yet seldom connect on a deeper level. The undercurrent of daily life pulls you into self-centeredness. The sin of selfishness can lead to isolation and destroy your marriage. However, by yielding our lives to Christ, who gave His life to rescue us from our selfish desires, we are able to build a strong and intimate marriage. Trust and dependence on God's love enable you to stay connected and committed not only when it's easy but for a lifetime. Again, we remind you that it is so worth it—marriage is remarkable!

GOD'S PLAN FOR INTIMACY

In Genesis 2:18-25, God saw that it was not good for a man to be alone. Even though Adam had a perfect environment, perfect position, and a perfect relationship with God, he was isolated.

The older I (Byron) get, the more I realize being fully vulnerable and "naked" emotionally and spiritually, as well as physically, brings about true intimacy—into-me-see (simple definition of intimacy).[17] Carla sees everything about my life and still accepts me. The beauty of the marriage covenant is that each individual promises never to leave nor forsake the other.

HOW DO ROMANCE AND INTIMACY ERODE?

Laziness can erode intimacy and romance. It is easy to take the faithfulness of your mate for granted. It is also easy to become lazy in meeting each other's needs, settling instead for the mundane and mediocre.

Early in marriage, tenderness, romance, and thoughtfulness are instinctive and come naturally. Later, though, they require discipline and commitment. For many couples, rather than spending the effort to meet each other's needs, the demands of careers, kids, and individual needs become the focus of the marriage.

HELPFUL SUGGESTIONS

A newly married couple can avoid the trap of laziness and truly seek to meet each other's needs by purposefully giving priority to time with one another each week. Other people and events will try to crowd out your time together. In making time for each other, you will say *no* to many very good things. But, you will be saying *yes* to maintaining an intimate, healthy marriage.

Work hard to become a student of your spouse. I am motivated to get a Ph.D. in "Carla-ology." Remember: women and men are very different in both their desires for intimacy and their ideas of romance.

It is important to openly and honestly communicate each of your desires. Both of you should strive to listen to each other, to truly understand each other's love language, and then begin to find creative ways of communicating love to one another. Never forget the incredible value of your spouse.

May the commitment you make at the altar "in sickness and in health, to love, honor, and cherish, till death do us part" become a reality as your love deepens over the years. Most of all, may you never bury your head in the newspaper on a dinner date!

TWO ROWBOATS

James Dobson tells the following story:

Imagine, if you will, two little rowboats [setting off to cross] a choppy lake. A man sits in one, a woman rides blissfully in the other. They have every intention of rowing side by side to the other shore, but then they begin drifting in opposite directions. They can hardly hear each other above the sound of the wind. Soon the man finds himself at the northern end of the lake, and the woman bobs along toward the south. Neither can recall how he or she drifted so far from the other or how to reconnect.

This simple illustration has meaning for couples who embark on life's journey. They stand at the altar and pledge to live together in love and harmony. Unfortunately, it doesn't always work that way. Unless their relationship is maintained and cultivated, it will grow distant and estranged. In a sense, this is why romantic little rowboats often drift toward opposite ends of the lake.

The question to be raised is, how can husbands and wives remain in the same proximity for a lifetime? The solution is for them to row like crazy. Take time for romantic activities. Think not of yourself but of the other. Avoid that which breeds conflict and resentment. And listen carefully to the needs of your partner. These are the keys to harmony and friendship.

It is difficult to keep two rowboats floating along together, but it can be done if each partner is determined to row. [18]

HEALTHY VS. UNHEALTHY RELATIONSHIPS
EXPECTATIONS[19]

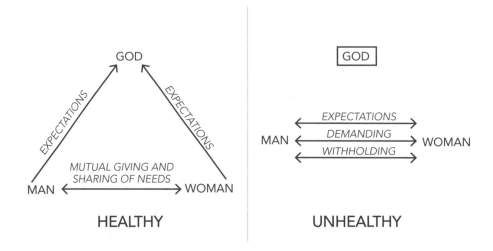

To understand the difference between healthy and unhealthy relationships, we focus on the issue of expectations. Who do you expect to meet your needs? Partners in a healthy relationship look to God for satisfaction and blessing. Partners in an unhealthy relationship expect another person to be their source of happiness. If you are in a healthy relationship in which God is meeting your needs, you can feel free to trust other people to the Lord. In other words, you may desire for your wife be more supportive as a helper, but your faith is that God can be trusted with both your needs and your wife. If your relationship is unhealthy, you will expect other people to please you; and when your needs are not met, you will likely become angry, demanding, and manipulative.[20]

SHARING NEEDS

In healthy relationships, couples express needs openly and in a loving way. For example, "I've been missing our time together. Can we plan a special date just the two of us?" Unhealthy relationships usually follow one of two extremes.

1. Not sharing the truth about our needs, hiding needs, becoming overly self-reliant

2. Sharing needs but not in a loving way.

GIVING VS. TAKING

Mutual giving is the key to healthy relationships. This relationship represents two people giving to meet their mates' important emotional needs and mutually receiving from one another. "It is more blessed to give than to receive" (Acts 20:35). Unhealthy relationships represent two emotionally bankrupt people trying desperately to take from each other. A codependent relationship is characterized by a very conditional love. "I'll love you if" or "I'll love when." This performance cycle is never ending, and it never satisfies.

SPIRITUAL INTIMACY

CAN TWO REALLY BECOME ONE SPIRITUALLY?

OVERVIEW

The purpose of this section is to encourage and challenge individuals to pursue godly character and discipline. We also hope to help couples relate on a spiritual basis as oneness occurs. As your relationship matures, spiritual oneness will be the foundation to emotional connection and physical passion.

"The sanctity of marriage necessitates personal commitment— necessity of commitment is weakened by our sinful nature; and our sinful nature can be counteracted by Jesus Christ."[1]

CHARLES SWINDOLL

"ACCORDING TO GOD'S HOLY ORDINANCES"

"When first things are put first, second things
are not suppressed but increased."[2]
C.S. LEWIS

SESSION GOAL

To encourage and challenge each partner to individually keep Christ as
the first priority and to grow together in spiritual oneness as a couple.

KEY BIBLICAL PRINCIPLES

- Psalm 1—Meditate on God's Word day and night.
- Psalm 119:9—The key to keep ourselves pure is to live according to God's Word and remain single-minded.
- Psalm 127:1—Unless the Lord builds the house, couples are just working tirelessly.
- Matthew 5:48; 1 Peter 1:14-16—Spiritual growth and development as a couple is dependent on individual spiritual growth and development.
- Romans 15:7—To really love our spouses, we must accept them just as God made them.

Dear Leader,

As you prepare to lead this session, please know how you organize your time largely depends on knowing where your couples are in their personal faith journeys. Your time together presents a great opportunity to clearly communicate the gospel and to boldly lead individuals to salvation through Jesus Christ. Pray for life change prior to your meeting.

Keep in mind, those who know Christ as Savior and Lord need to hear the challenge of Psalm 127:1, "Unless the LORD builds the house, the builders labor in vain."

Every couple needs to realize that salvation is immediate, but sanctification takes a lifetime. Remind them that spiritual growth and development as a couple is one hundred percent dependent on individual spiritual growth and development. Most married couples come to realize in time that "iron sharpens iron" (Prov. 27:17). They learn to appreciate what the other person contributes to the marriage, and they find a healthy balance of pursuing God together.

To Have and To Hold is designed as a tool to pass biblical principles from one generation to the next. Marriage is one of the greatest ways to demonstrate the gospel message of Christ being united with the bridegroom in oneness.

We are daily able to live that out in marriage. What an honor.

Most of us are looking for a simple formula we can use to follow God's holy ordinances. Sadly, many Christians are just religious enough to be miserable, making God's ordinances legalities that exasperate us. As religious people, we live with a certain amount of traditional, ceremonial, and dogmatic behavior. We do it automatically. When we were children, we were taught to behave and even think in a prescribed way. If we're simply going through the motions, do we really experience spiritual growth when we go to church, do good deeds, pray, make good moral decisions, meditate, and so forth? To answer that question, it is important to attempt to define *spiritual growth*.

Traditional ways can be important to the process, but true spiritual growth occurs when the Spirit of God is made known in our lives and our egos shrink. In some ways, spiritual growth is a misnomer. The Spirit does not grow or shrink; He remains the way He is, never changing. Further, spiritual growth happens only in direct relationship to a diminishing of our ego. The ego refers to my self-centered qualities that determine decisions based solely on what is best for me. My reasoning is based upon my needs—I, I, I, me, me, me. In contrast, for true spiritual growth to occur, we must come to realize that God is the center of the universe—not me, my marriage, or my wedding. We should probably rename this section *ego diminishing*. Entering into a marriage covenant is a great way to experience ego shrinkage.

If someone had pulled us aside during our engagement and told us that living out this part of the marriage vow would be one of the greatest challenges to oneness in our marriage, we would have denied it. But, when the honeymoon was over, we began to realize the complexity of growing together in Christ. Reluctantly we have recognized that our struggle is due to individual selfishness, ego, and pride. Spiritual growth takes place daily—adding to the difficulty. In other areas, such as money, in-laws, and even communication, you can usually take a break for a couple of days. But, spiritual growth is so dynamic, it demands constant attention and learning about one another.

As this session challenges you to pursue godly character and discipline, our hope is that spiritual oneness will occur. Only when you begin to understand yourself and, more importantly, God will you begin to understand and experience how two can really become one spiritually.

PREP WORK
(10 minutes)

How did working through the Bible study book go this week?

STARTER QUESTIONS FROM THE BIBLE STUDY BOOK WILL LEAD INTO THE SESSION.

If you could ask God any question about life and marriage, what would it be?

As a (soon-to-be) married person, what would you receive spiritually from marriage that you would not as a single person?

How has Christ impacted your life? Share how and when Christ became the center of your life.

TRANSITIONAL QUESTION: In your opinion, how does a person measure whether he or she is growing spiritually?

STATE THE PART OF THE VOWS AND PRESENT THE KEY QUESTION (P. 87) FOR THIS SECTION.

PRAY.

DRIVING QUESTIONS

(40 minutes)

WHAT IS SPIRITUAL GROWTH?

> God's love is the only love that is strong enough
> to maintain a marriage relationship.

HOW DOES A PERSON MEASURE SPIRITUAL GROWTH?

As the couple(s) answer the transitional question about measuring spiritual growth, keep in mind that most of us within the church evaluate spiritual growth by "what we do" not by "who and whose we are." Instead, let's approach it this way: spiritual growth is measured by pursuing God and imitating Christ (and learning to die to self as discussed earlier—ego diminishing). Perhaps a better question to ask is:

How does God measure spiritual growth? Why is it important in marriage?

What do you think the phrase "discipline brings freedom" means?

As the Holy Spirit works in each of our lives, we need to accept the responsibility to obey and follow God's transformational path toward a new life. This will require discipline.

The root word of *disciple* is "discipline." *Disciple* simply means to become a learner or a pupil.[3]

As learners, we are constantly gaining new knowledge that shines light onto the path we are called to walk. Learning does not simply happen on its own. It requires inquiry, discovery, and experiencing truth that is based on reality.

WHY ARE SPIRITUAL DISCIPLINES IMPORTANT IN A MARRIAGE?

One of the ways our early church leaders modeled life was through the practice of spiritual disciplines such as:

- *Silence*
- *Solitude*
- *Sabbath Rest*
- *Prayer*
- *Fasting*
- *Bible study*

Today many of us associate Sunday or Sabbath with a focus on the sacred, yet God desires for His children to live a holy life every day. We cannot separate the sacred from the secular. In our attempt to compartmentalize Christianity, we have often reduced it down to empty religious activity.

How would you define spiritual formation?
Why is it important in a marriage?

Is it easy or difficult to pray with one another? Why?

Within a marriage, each of us is daily reminded of how self-seeking we are in life. This is why we need a Savior.

Commitment is another reason why we need a Savior. In our relationship with Christ, we will find the motivation and strength to keep a marriage commitment when the going gets tough. We cannot drum up enough motivation and strength on our own—it won't happen.

As a couple, how much does the Bible inform the principles that guide your lives?

DO YOU RELATE TO GOD IN THE SAME WAY?

Helping couples understand the importance of being on the same page spiritually begins by better understanding how each draws near to God.

Ask each couple to turn to "How We Relate to God." (See The Tools, p.100.) It describes nine possible temperaments from which we relate to God.[4] Have couples identify the one or two pathways that resonate with them personally. We are not talking about beliefs but the manner in which a couple worships and pursues Jesus Christ. Have the couple discuss the similarities and differences between each partner's preferences and approach to God.

NOTE: All of these temperaments are built upon the basic assumption that the way to God the Father is through Jesus Christ.

Do each of you relate to God in the same way?

What do you desire from your mate regarding spiritual connection?

What could you do to help yourself worship more deeply on a regular basis?

WHY IS SPIRITUAL ONENESS THE FOUNDATION OF A HEALTHY MARRIAGE AND HOME?

Spiritual oneness has been proven to:

- Deepen your conversation and thought level with one another.

- Deepen your intimacy with one another.

- Increase your commitment and compatibility with one another.

- Increase your capacity to express love for one another.

"He is before all things, and in him all things hold together."
COLOSSIANS 1:17

CONFLICT AND STRUGGLES—CHAOS

Marriage has a way of multiplying trials, conflicts, and struggles—often leading to chaos. Keep in mind, however, one of the greatest educational tools is dis-equilibrium. When we're thrown off balance, we work hard to come back to center and find balance. During these times of chaos, we have a greater potential to empty ourselves (ego diminishing), leaving room for a filling of God's Spirit.

In life, receptacles must be emptied before they may be filled again. Read Philippians 2:5-11. We should take on this attitude of humility as we respond to our spouses.

OTHER THOUGHT-PROVOKING QUESTIONS TO ASK COUPLES

Leading couples into spiritual oneness has many dimensions. Here are some great discussion questions to help them think through how two people can become one spiritually:

What does it mean to be a spiritual leader? Is spiritual leadership solely the responsibility of the husband? How does one become a spiritual leader?

Why do most young couples wait until after their children come along to connect with a local church?

How involved in a local church do you plan to be? Are you on the same page with your (future) spouse regarding church participation? Why or why not? What would it take to be on the same page?

Why is physical passion tied so closely to spiritual oneness?

"So here's what I want you to do, God helping you: Take your everyday, ordinary life—your sleeping, eating, going-to-work, and walking-around life—and place it before God as an offering. Embracing what God does for you is the best thing you can do for him. Don't become so well-adjusted to your culture that you fit into it without even thinking. Instead, fix your attention on God. You'll be changed from the inside out. Readily recognize what he wants from you, and quickly respond to it. Unlike the culture around you, always dragging you down to its level of immaturity, God brings the best out of you, develops well-formed maturity in you ... The only accurate way to understand ourselves is by what God is and by what he does for us, not by what we are and what we do for him."

ROMANS 12:1-3, *THE MESSAGE*

Refer to Prep Work Assignment #4 in the Bible study book. Challenge couples to select two or three ways to work toward developing spiritual maturity as a couple.

Conclude by setting aside a time for couples to pray together. This prayer time may be uncomfortable for some, or a daily pattern for others that might appear boring, but everyone can greatly benefit.

A WORD OF CAUTION

The more a couple prays together, the closer they become. Advise couples to be cautious and intentional to guard their physical purity during their engagement. Couples wonder why it is so difficult during engagement to control their physical passions. The physical body does not know the difference between being married or unmarried, but the spirit, mind, and emotion certainly know the distinction.

It is good to grow in spiritual oneness. But be aware that the more the spirit and soul connect in oneness, the more quickly the body's natural reactions will follow.

This session can be one of the most foundational in *To Have and To Hold*. As you encourage and challenge individuals to pursue godly character and discipline on their own, pray from them to grasp the crucial nature of spiritually connecting as a couple.

It is important that couples clearly demonstrate the oneness of Christ and the church. It's this picture of the bride joining her bridegroom that helps our neighborhood better comprehend Christ and the church. The church needs deeply committed marriages, and our cities need faithful churches.

With the privilege of marriage comes great responsibility. Personally living according to God's holy ordinances is the greatest thing you can do for your marriage.

SYNOPSIS

In my life, I (Byron) can point to three areas that have assisted me in diminishing my ego and, thus, growing spiritually. Developing personal discipline, attempting to understand true *agape* love, and struggling through hardship have deepened my faith in Jesus Christ as I strived to live according to God's holy ordinances. In the process, Carla and I have sharpened one another as "iron sharpens iron" (Prov. 27:17). We have learned to appreciate each other's qualities and have found a healthy balance in pursuing God together. We have found again and again in our marriage that our relationships with God are foundational to our journey toward oneness.

PERSONAL DISCIPLINE AS AN AVENUE TO ONENESS

A year and a half after our wedding, my faith journey felt like I was sprinting on a treadmill. Spiritually, I was working harder and moving faster, doing things religiously, yet not making any ground in knowing, understanding, and living out biblical principles. I was so busy doing things for God and attempting to impress God that I completely missed God in the process. *Ordering Your Private World* by Gordon MacDonald changed my approach to life. For the first time in my life as a Christian, I realized that discipline brings freedom. As I began to practice inner spiritual disciplines, God's Spirit changed my life.

Over the years I have observed that busyness is one of the biggest distractions to growing in Christ. Busy, busy, busy. I am *so busy*! *Merriam-Webster's* dictionary defines *busy* as being "engaged in action; full of activity; foolishly or intrusively active; or full of distracting detail."[5] If we are not careful, busyness can easily become cluttered activity with minute detail that distracts us from the focal point. Did you catch that? Cluttered activity that distracts attention from the focal point.

In order to make Christ a major priority in your life, and thus your marriage, you must eliminate the cluttered activity that distracts you from the focal point—Jesus Christ is our focus. The disciplines of prayer, Bible study, fasting, Sabbath rest, solitude, and simplicity can take you off the treadmill and move you forward toward gainful activity.

UNDERSTANDING TRUE LOVE AS
AN AVENUE TO ONENESS

As I strive to become less egocentric and more Christ-focused, I realize how much my marriage relationship facilitates my spiritual growth. My relationship with Carla is a constant opportunity for me to live out the truths I believe about God. I can't drum up enough feeling or motivation to love Carla long-term without being empowered by the Holy Spirit. God's Spirit enables me to comprehend patience, kindness, goodness, faithfulness, gentleness, and self-control. If these qualities, listed in Galatians 5:22-23, are let loose in our lives, then we experience oneness in marriage.

ONENESS BENEFITS

As you consider growing in the knowledge of Christ, there are no easy conditional formulas of "do this and then this will happen." Spiritual growth will be one of the toughest issues you face in your marriage because it requires dying to self. But the perks of spiritual oneness are well worth the sacrifice. As part of you diminishes, it is replaced with character qualities from an Almighty God.

As the two of you take on Christlike qualities, you will experience life change. Spiritual oneness:

- Deepens your conversation and thought level with one another.

- Deepens your intimacy with one another.

- Increases your commitment and compatibility with one another.

- Increases your capacity to express love for one another.

Personally living according to God's holy ordinances is the greatest thing you can do for your marriage.

HOW WE RELATE TO GOD
Adapted from **Sacred Pathways** *by* **Gary Thomas**

NATURALISTS: LOVING GOD OUT OF DOORS

"Naturalists seek God by surrounding themselves with all that He has made." They "would prefer to leave any building, however beautiful, to pray to God beside a river [or a lake.]"[6] Jesus loved to use creation as a tool to teach truths of God. An example can be found in the parable of the sower and seed in Matthew 13:2-23.

SENSATES: LOVING GOD WITH THE SENSES

"Sensate Christians want to be lost in the awe, beauty, and splendor of God. When these Christians worship, they want to be filled with sights, sounds, and smells that overwhelm them."[7] The five senses are God's most effective inroad to their hearts. We see in the fourteenth chapter of Mark (vv. 3-9) a woman anointing Jesus with perfume. Because we know it was very expensive, the smell of the fragrance must have been beautiful!

TRADITIONALISTS: LOVING GOD THROUGH RITUAL AND SYMBOL

"Traditionalists are fed by what are often termed the historic dimensions of faith: rituals, symbols, sacraments and sacrifice. These Christians tend to have a disciplined life of faith. Frequently they enjoy regular attendance at church services, tithing, keeping the Sabbath, and so on. Traditionalists have a need for ritual and structure."[8] Jesus instituted the practice of the Lord's Supper Himself as we see recorded in the fourteenth chapter of Mark's gospel (vv. 12-26). He instructed His disciples (then and today) to follow His example and to do this in remembrance of me" (1 Cor. 11:24).

ASCETICS: LOVING GOD IN SOLITUDE AND SIMPLICITY

"Ascetics want nothing more than to be left alone in prayer. They are uncomfortable in any environment that keeps them from listening to the quiet."[9] "Very early in the morning, while it was still dark, Jesus got up, left the house and went off to a solitary place, where he prayed" (Mark 1:35).

ACTIVISTS: LOVING GOD THROUGH CONFRONTATION

"Activists serve a God of justice, and their favorite Scripture is often the account of Jesus cleansing the temple. They define *worship* as standing against evil and calling sinners to repentance. These Christians often view the church as a place to recharge their batteries so they can go back into the world to wage war against injustice."[10] A wonderful example in Scripture of loving God through confrontation can be found in the fourth chapter of Matthew when Jesus confronts Satan in the wilderness.

CAREGIVERS: LOVING GOD BY LOVING OTHERS

"Caregivers serve God by serving others. They often claim to see Christ in the poor and needy, and their faith is built up by interacting with other people. Whereas caring for others might wear many of us down, this recharges a caregiver's batteries."[11] Throughout Scripture, especially in the Gospels, we can see Jesus expressing his love for others by caring for their physical needs. In Matthew 8, we see Jesus healing the sick. However, His ultimate act of love can be found in His death on the cross.

ENTHUSIASTS: LOVING GOD WITH MYSTERY AND CELEBRATION

"Excitement and mystery in worship is the spiritual lifeblood of enthusiasts. These Christians are cheerleaders for God and the Christian life. They don't want to just know concepts, but to experience them, to feel them, and to be moved by them."[12] One place in Scripture where there can be found both celebration of God and yet an underlying mysterious awe is definitely in the telling of Jesus' birth.

CONTEMPLATIVES: LOVING GOD THROUGH ADORATION

The contemplative seeks to know the personhood of God and to be caught up in pursuing a loving experience with God. "Contemplatives refer to God as their lover, and images of a loving Father and Bridegroom predominate their view of God. These Christians seek to love God with the purest, deepest, and brightest love imaginable."[13] We see in the account of Luke (10:38-42) where Jesus commends Mary of Bethany as she sat and worshipped at his feet, simply by "being still and knowing" Him (Ps. 46:10).

INTELLECTUALS: LOVING GOD WITH THE MIND

"Intellectuals might be skeptics or committed believers, but in either case they are likely to be studying. These Christians live in the world of concepts. They may feel closest to God when they first understand something new about him. 'Faith' is something to be understood as much as experienced."[14] Luke gives us the best example of loving God with the mind in chapter two, where Jesus, as a young boy, is found "in the temple courts, sitting among the teachers, listening to them and asking them questions" (v. 46).

PHYSICAL INTIMACY

HOW DO WE ACHIEVE SEXUAL INTIMACY?

OVERVIEW

The purpose of this section is to educate couples regarding various aspects, myths, and expectations of sexual intimacy. "And they shall become one flesh" (Gen. 2:24, NASB).

"Getting married for sex is like buying a 747 for the peanuts."[1]

JEFF FOXWORTHY

"THE TWO SHALL BECOME ONE FLESH."

> "We should not be ashamed to discuss that
> which God was not ashamed to create."[2]
> **DR. HOWARD HENDRICKS**

SESSION GOAL

To provide open discussion and educate couples regarding the factors, myths, and expectations of sexual intimacy.

KEY BIBLICAL PRINCIPLES

- Genesis 1:27-28; 3:20—God created sexuality.
- Genesis 1:28; 2:24; Matthew 19:5-6—Sex within the covenant of marriage is holy, good, and encouraged.
- Song of Solomon 4:10—Sexuality is designed by God to provide pleasure.
- 1 Corinthians 7:2-5—Sex should take place consistently between a husband and a wife.
- 1 Thessalonians 4:4-5; Philippians 2:4; 1 Corinthians 7:3-5— One's sexuality is not to be self-oriented but other-oriented.
- Hebrews 13:4—The marriage bed is honorable.

Dear Leader,

*Sharing sexual intimacy with a spouse is something that only a marital partner can give. No one else has the right or privilege to share this act. Others can give gifts, hang out with one another, or even share conversation, but **no one** except a spouse is honored to be able to share sexual intimacy.*

Teaching this session may prove difficult because you are balancing a fine line between educating and invading private space. Yet, in order to help couples gain more freedom, it is necessary to identify distortions and replace some of the cultural lies with God's view of sex.

Whenever sexual intimacy is given the connotation of being dirty, nasty, or evil, we must recognize this as a lie and distortion of God's perfect creation. These distorted thoughts are frequently born out of a human's twisted view of physical intimacy—a view which often involves premarital, extramarital, or perverted relationships used to fulfill a self-centered physical desire.

These distortions can come from a cultural Christianity that miscommunicates the sinful side of human sexuality. Often within the Christian culture it is easier to declare all of human sexuality as wrong and bad rather than to deal with it honestly. Please consider dealing with this topic honestly.

Thank you for helping couples discover exciting, deeper levels of intimacy.

"Sex is a total body experience—not a contact sport."
ANONYMOUS

Statistics indicate the average couple experiences sex two to three times per week.[3] When most men enter marriage, their sexual expectations are much higher than the average. Honestly, my (Byron) picture of our honeymoon and first years of marriage included having sex all or most of every day. But three children and several years into marriage, I would have modified the statistical evidence to read "two to three times per week, if they are fortunate—and don't have small children."

One young man in our class took it on as a personal challenge to increase the national statistical average of time spent in sexual activity. The truth is that sex is only a fraction of the whole sum of marriage. Although a small part, sexual intimacy is a powerful, exciting, and significant component that brings intimacy with your spouse to new levels.

There are 168 hours in a week and the average couple spends only a small portion of that time in sexual activity. It did not take me long as a new husband to realize that those one to two hours of sexual activity a week were completely dependent on the other 166. Rest, nutrition, stress, work schedules, money concerns, communication, spiritual attitudes, dirty clothes, dishwashing, and giving one another undivided attention, among other things, all factor into the equation. Certainly, the non-sexual activities of the day are vital for a couple to experience meaningful, sexual intimacy.

Obviously, God created male and female distinctly different. Both men and women have sexual desires, but making love meets these needs in a different way for each partner. Comedian Jerry Seinfeld accurately states, "The basic conflict between men and women, sexually, is that men are like firemen. To men, sex is an emergency, and no matter what we're doing we can be ready in two minutes. Women, on the other hand, are like fire. They're very exciting, but the conditions have to be exactly right."[4]

CONFORMING TO THE PATTERNS OF THIS WORLD

Although sex is a hot topic in our society, I am convinced most of us have been misinformed and/or undereducated regarding human sexuality. Most men and women lack a good factual understanding of the issues pertaining to a healthy sexual relationship with their spouses. In addition, many myths continue to be passed on as truth. Undereducation and misinformation serve as barriers, or at least hindrances, to our fully experiencing what God created to be a sanctified, sexual relationship.

Thus, it is critical to grasp that God created sexual intimacy to be a beautiful and sacred part of the husband and wife relationship. Our physical bodies and the act of physical love are the pure and divine creations of a perfect and loving God. The biblical premise of God's perfect creation forms the foundation of any discussion about our sensual natures. Therefore, any time human sexuality is given a dirty or nasty connotation, we must understand it as a lie and a distortion of God's creation.

In contradiction to God's truth, our cultural misinformation encourages premarital, extramarital, or perverted sexual relationships. The Bible gives specific instruction to avoid such relationships. This instruction is designed to protect and provide for us in order that we might experience true intimacy with others. God created us to need real, life-giving, intimate relationships—not selfish, physical passion that deceives and robs us of life.

Before you physically consummate the marriage, it is vital for you to use your brain to think through truths, myths, and expectations. As this session prepares the two of you to become one flesh, be sure—for now—only your mind and your soul are brought to the discussion.

PREP WORK
(10 minutes)

How did working through the Bible study book go this week?

STARTER QUESTIONS FROM THE BIBLE STUDY BOOK WILL LEAD INTO THE SESSION.

HELPFUL TIP: *If you're using this material in a group setting, divide the class time into three parts: 1) teach and discuss with the entire group; 2) conduct frank gender discussion with males and females separately; and 3) bring the whole group back together for a final challenge.*

Did you enjoy Prep Work #1 Assignment in your Bible study book?

NOTE: *Remind couples to develop a plan to keep themselves pure.*

Did you review the sexual intimacy questions? (These can be found in the appendix of the Bible study book or online at LifeWay.com/ToHaveAndToHold.) What are some of your observations?

What was it like talking about this topic together?

TRANSITIONAL QUESTION: Why do you think so many people are confused about sex? Why are there so many myths and misunderstandings surrounding sex?

STATE THE BIBLICAL PRINCIPLE AND PRESENT THE KEY QUESTION (P. 103) FOR THIS SECTION.

PRAY.

IS OUR CULTURE SENDING CONFUSING MESSAGES ABOUT SEX?

In our culture, sex is a hot topic, yet oftentimes couples have been both miseducated and undereducated regarding human sexuality.

Both undereducation and miseducation serve as barriers or at least hindrances to experiencing the fullness of what God created to be a sanctified, sexual relationship. Through an open and honest discussion, we hope that you, as a leader, can challenge couples to seek God's will in this exciting new area of their relationship as husband and wife. As you prepare for this discussion, consider the following thoughts. Begin this section with more general discussion questions in order to set the tone.

Why do you think our society is consumed with sex?

Is it possible that we have been both miseducated and undereducated about human sexuality? How?

Why do many Christians have trouble giving themselves permission to celebrate and have a great time in the sensuous pleasures of married love?

Jesus addressed the divine relationship of sexual intimacy—the spiritual and physical joining together of husband and wife as one flesh. Listen to what He says in Matthew:

> "Haven't you read," he replied, "that at the beginning the Creator 'made them male and female,' and said, 'For this reason a man will leave his father and mother and be united to his wife, and the two will become one flesh'? So they are no longer two, but one flesh. Therefore what God has joined together, let no one separate."
> **MATTHEW 19:4-6**

Jesus directly addresses the marriage relationship as "one flesh." This refers to intimacy in the partially the sensual, sexual way He created us.

There is a certain amount of security in the phrase "what God has joined together, let no one separate" (Matt. 19:6). That could be why Paul spoke in Hebrews 13:4 about keeping the marriage "honored by all, and the marriage bed kept pure."

"ONE FLESH" IS A LEARNING PROCESS.

In order to find security in the sexual relationship of a marriage, couples need a basic understanding of sexuality. Please help couples to realize that if they are married fifty years, they will have 18,250 nights together. This realization should help couples feel less pressure on "the first night" and help them to relax, laugh, and enjoy being married, naked, and unashamed!

Research shows that the average couple will have sex two to three times a week.[5] These few hours spent in sexual activity are completely dependent on the other 166 hours of normal life throughout the week.

God created male and female bodies such that making love is an indescribable experience. It should be viewed as a special gift from a loving Father who desires men and women to become one flesh, giving themselves to one another not only spiritually and emotionally, but also physically.

How can our sex lives teach us valuable lessons in our spiritual lives?

What is one sexual myth you have believed in the past?

HINDRANCES TO THE LEARNING PROCESS

Couples who are preparing to examine sexual intimacy should be made aware of several noteworthy hindrances.

The media brainwashes us to think that sexual intimacy just happens beautifully without problems. In reality, it is more of a trial and error process.

Research shows that for an average man to have an orgasm, it takes three to five minutes of direct or indirect stimulation.[6] And for an average female, it will take fifteen to forty minutes to reach orgasm—and that's once the female mind and emotion have warmed up and communicated with the physical.[7]

Some individuals are selfish in their sexuality, using phrases and attitudes like "Getting it!" and "Doing it!" regarding sexual intimacy with a spouse. Sex is not "getting some" because this implies that sex is like a material possession. Sex is not "doing it" either. If it's "doing it" then sex becomes a performance trap of how well you acted. It's an activity judged by your performance and your performance alone. These terms are not appropriate because they do not take into account the deep, spiritual connection that you and your spouse maintain. God has brought you together as one. Along with that oneness, you are to care for, honor, and respect your spouse as yourself. Our perspectives and speech regarding sexual intimacy should always reflect a heart of love and consideration. We have to change our mind-set and really consider others as more important than ourselves.

Couples need to understand that sexual intimacy is not a seven-minute experience. Sexual intimacy is an all-day affair. Some men are more aggressive and experience pleasure more quickly. Many women have trouble giving themselves permission to celebrate and have a great time in the sensuous pleasures of married love.

Christians find it challenging to construct a definition of being "godly" while including words like *sexual* and *sensuous*. In some Christian minds, in order to become godly, they must deny their sensuality. As a result, they have robbed themselves and their spouses of one of God's greatest gifts—the ability to delight in physical union as husband and wife.

HELPFUL TIP: *As a leader, find balance between candid openness and protecting your privacy. Do not invite these couples into the privacy of your sex life—that is between you and your spouse.*

At this point, divide the women and men to separately discuss some of the hindrances facing newlyweds. Create an open environment for a candid discussion. Please see the following discussion topics for "Men Only" and for "Women Only."

Work to lay the foundation for a safe environment. Allow the women and men to ask questions and lead themselves in the discussion.

WHAT ARE SOME HINDRANCES YOU SEE FACING NEWLYWEDS?

Why do you think God make men and women so differently in how long it takes them to become sexually stimulated?

Do you wish you had a better understanding of healthy sexual relationships? Where did you learn the most about sex?

If one person in a marital relationship is more willing to learn about sex than the other, what does this tell you?

What unhealthy messages did you receive about sex when you were younger?

What questions do you have?

FOR WOMEN ONLY:

CONSIDER COVERING THESE TOPICS WITH THE WOMEN:

- *Misunderstandings women face*
- *Tendency to adopt mother's attitude toward sex*
- *Frequency of husband's sexual desire*
- *Three keys to sexual thinking pattern:*
    - *What she thinks about lovemaking*
    - *What she thinks about herself*
    - *What she thinks about her husband*
- *Transition into "naked and not ashamed"*
- *Discuss previous experience, thoughts, and struggles.*
- *Discuss initial sexual experience: will it hurt?*
- *Communication: Telling one another what is pleasing—a tough but necessary discussion.*
- *Birth control*
- *Male premature ejaculation*
- *Clean up after sex.*
- *Practice self-control.*

FOR MEN ONLY:

CONSIDER COVERING THESE TOPICS WITH THE MEN:

- *Non-sexual touching arouses a woman. A satisfying sexual relationship grows out of a satisfying personal relationship.*
- *Be patient, move at her pace, do not rush lovemaking.*
- *Transition into "naked and not ashamed." Remind males they are not in a dorm or a locker room—it's important to be very respectful.*
- *Discuss previous experience, thoughts, and struggles.*
- *Discuss initial sexual experience.*
- *Communication: Telling one another what is pleasing—a tough but necessary discussion.*
- *Birth control*
- *Premature ejaculation*
- *Clean up after sex.*
- *Practice self-control.*
- *Pornography*

WHAT SHOULD WE EXPECT ON OUR WEDDING NIGHT?

What are you most looking forward to on your wedding night?

Read "The Wedding Night" found in Song of Solomon 4:1–5:1. As you read these poetic words, what insight did you gain?

TO BETTER UNDERSTAND ONE ANOTHER

In her surveys, social researcher Shaunti Feldhahn discussed how husbands and wives feel about physical intimacy.

Roughly fifty-five percent of women said they wanted sex more often or exactly the same as their husbands. Yet, it appears that the majority of men believe their wives desire sex "less often."[8]

As stated earlier, women desire to be cherished. Men may not realize how physical intimacy is closely tied to this.

When asked why they tend to want sex less than their husband, the vast majority said "it's not that [they] don't want to be with him"—it's just a difficult transition from a long day or sometimes they are simply too tired or stressed.[9]

Many women think that all men want is sex. However, men are so much more complex than that. Often men don't know how to cognitively understand what is going on in their needs for physical intimacy, much less are they able to verbally articulate those emotions to their spouses. Wives may not realize that what happens in the bedroom impacts a man's emotional well-being and self-perception. Regular sexual intimacy actually gives men a greater sense of worth, value, and satisfaction with life.

It's an emotional need that men can't meet in any other way.[10]

Research shows that many men long for the heart connection that comes with sexual intimacy.[11]

Realistically, most men greatly desire sex. But women do too when they are nurtured and cared for. Keep in mind, there are deeper emotional needs at play. Men are more complex than people give them credit for.

The bottom line: both men and women really do long for a heart connect. Both men and women physically enjoy the pleasures of sex. We are wired that way!

Are there any considerations we need to take into account to enhance our first sexual experience?

What can we do to keep from being so exhausted on the week of our wedding?

If you are married for fifty years, you will have 18,250 nights together. How does this realization take the pressure off of "the first night?" What are some ways you can relax, laugh, and enjoy being married, naked, and unashamed?

BAGGAGE BROUGHT INTO THE RELATIONSHIP

In our culture today, it is rare for couples to enter marriage without some sort of baggage caused by confusing messages or past hurts. There can be a great amount of guilt and shame associated with sexuality.

If you have had sex before, how do you deal with the fact that this is not your first time? How can you make your wedding night special as you consummate your marriage?

PAST HURTS

Byron's doctoral research indicated that only twenty-seven percent of Christian couples (mind you, Christian couples who came from Christian families) entered the marriage bed chaste or pure.

It is important to the future of a marital relationship for a person to come clean with God and receive a second chance in sexual purity. Do-overs are important in life. We must be honest enough with ourselves to confess that we have pursued self and not God in the area of sex. Repent and receive the undeserved grace and forgiveness that a holy God offers through Jesus Christ.

Repentance will re-establish purity in the mental and physical areas of a person's life. God is about forgiveness. God is about confession. He wants us to admit that, although natural, our own selfish behavior is incredibly destructive to us and others.

> "If we confess our sins, he is faithful and just to forgive us
> our sins and to cleanse us from all unrighteousness."
> **1 JOHN 1:9, ESV**

First John 1:8, says, "If we claim to be without sin, we deceive ourselves." Not a single person in this world has it all together. Sexual sins are destructive, but just as with all other sin, God can repair and make whole the broken pieces left in the wake of the destructive path. Jesus Christ came to give us life and to make us whole.

The vast majority of the couples who attend a marriage prep course are in great need for God to heal past hurts. Couples must allow God to deal individually with the baggage in their lives as they prepare for both the honeymoon and marriage.

In *A Celebration of Sex for Newlyweds,* a pastor pleaded, "Just because they have already had sex, don't let [couples] treat their wedding night in an ordinary way. This is their first time of truly making love. Let them build on their new covenant as they discover exciting and deeper levels of sexual intimacy."[12]

DO YOU HAVE A PLAN TO REMAIN PHYSICALLY PURE?
If you are virgins, should we wait until we are married for your sexual relationship? If you have been sexually active as a couple, is it important that you stop sexual activity until after your wedding? Do you know what the Lord says about this in His Word?

"For this is the will of God, your sanctification: that you abstain from sexual immorality; that each one of you know how to control his own body in holiness and honor, not in the passion of lust like the Gentiles who do not know God; that no one transgress and wrong his brother in this matter, because the Lord is an avenger in all these things, as we told you beforehand and solemnly warned you. For God has not called us for impurity, but in holiness."

1 THESSALONIANS 4:3-8, ESV

Read 1 Thessalonians 4:3-8 above. Why do you think that the writer speaks about sanctification and sex in the same passage? What does it look like to abstain from sexual immorality?

How do you plan to control your own body now? Throughout your marriage?

In the 1 Thessalonians 4:3-8 passage, the word *abstain* means to "hold oneself off; refrain."[13] It implies to hold off, keep your feet on the ground, and reach for the choice fruit. Individuals must learn to control their bodies. This does not get any easier within marriage.

Challenge couples to use caution during their engagements. Our physical bodies do not know the difference in being married or not, but our minds, emotions, and spirits know there is a big difference. As the mind, emotion, and spirit draw closer, the physical will naturally follow. That is why we need a supernatural God (Holy Spirit) protecting us during this time. Staying sexually pure doesn't solely mean abstaining from sex outside of marriage. We should also examine other aspects of our lives (the media we consume, relationships we're involved in, places we frequent) to make sure they are pleasing to God and would not potentially open us up for sexual temptation.

What are your beliefs about pornography? Has pornography ever been a part of your life? If so, how recently? Take time to have an honest conversation with one another. How can your marriage partner help you in this area?

HOW WILL SEX INFLUENCE OUR FUTURE?

Do we really understand what a healthy sexual relationship looks like? How can this affect our future?

Is it important for what happens in the bedroom to stay in the bedroom?

How many children would we like to have someday? How long should we wait before we try to get pregnant?

Have we discussed birth control with one another and our physicians? What are our options?

How would a baby change our lives?

CONCLUSION

As you bring the couples back together, challenge them to:

1. *Work hard to better understand how their mates are wired.*
2. *Remain physically pure until their wedding days.*
3. *Plan relaxing honeymoons to take the pressure off the wedding night/honeymoon.*

HONEYMOON TIPS

- Before the wedding, talk through your expectations of the wedding night.

- Plan to rest the first day or two. Take the stress off of having sex.

- Plan your travel so that you can sleep in and have a relaxed morning the day after your wedding.

- Break the barrier of "naked and not ashamed" respectfully.

- Think through your honeymoon objectives. Do not plan to see all of Europe in a week. Instead, spend time together transitioning into oneness.

God created sex to be an incredible blessing for a husband and wife to enjoy. The key is to help couples understand how to meet one another's needs as they "consider others as more important than [them]selves" (Phil. 2:3, CSB). The session is about more than physical intimacy. The physical act of lovemaking connects the emotional and spiritual components for a married couple to find true intimacy.

The more a married couple understands the myths and expectations of their partners, the better the sex. As Christians, we should never be ashamed to openly discuss what God creatively designed.

PRAYER OF PROTECTION

The enemy is trying to steal, kill, and destroy the family (John 10:10). So why wouldn't he use this area to confuse, frustrate, and rip up a marriage. Couples need the Holy Spirit's protection.

Conclude by praying this prayer, based upon 1 Corinthians 10:13, over the couples.

"Oh God, please do not allow temptation to overtake each of these beautiful couples. We know that it is common for man to struggle sexually; yet, we know that You, Oh God, are faithful. You will not allow us to be tempted beyond what we can withstand; but with the temptation, You will provide the way of escape so that we will be able to endure it."

"The two will become one flesh" (Mark 10:8) is the most creative gift God has given to husband and wife. Let's maintain the sacredness of this relationship.

It is indeed a blessing to experience the fullness married life has to offer.

SYNOPSIS

God designed the wonderful blessing of physical intimacy to be a gift freely given to one's spouse. The key is that you give freely, no strings attached, to meet your spouse's needs. It is not something you do ("Did you do it?") or get ("Did you get some?") but something you share and give. This kind of giving is motivated by unconditional love. In 1 Corinthians 7:3-5, Paul speaks frankly about the issue of lovemaking when he indicates neither spouse has ownership over his or her own body in the marriage relationship. Rather, they are each to give of themselves to the other partner as there is need.

> "The husband should fulfill his marital duty to his wife, and likewise the wife to her husband. The wife does not have authority over her own body but yields it to her husband. In the same way, the husband does not have authority over his own body but yields it to his wife. Do not deprive each other except perhaps by mutual consent and for a time, so that you may devote yourselves to prayer. Then come together again so that Satan will not tempt you because of your lack of self-control."
>
> **1 CORINTHIANS 7:3-5**

If, however, one or both spouses begin to withhold the enjoyment of sexual intimacy from the other, tension and eventually some degree of bitterness could develop in the relationship. To avoid miscommunication, it is imperative for each spouse to communicate openly and honestly about physical desires and needs.

Also, within marriage, sexual relations are to be regular. As verse five says, "come together again so that Satan will not tempt you because of your lack of self-control." Although there is no ideal number of times per week, month, or year for a couple to engage in sexual intimacy, a guiding principle is to sexually "come together" regularly in order to meet your needs and you are not tempted to look elsewhere for sexual fulfillment.

IT LASTS A LIFETIME.

Lastly, learn to be patient with one another. You have a lifetime to enjoy each other sexually. Our culture would like to convince you that sexually everything takes place naturally, but this is a half-truth. More realistically, sexual intimacy it is a trial and error process that develops over the course of your marriage. In other words, do not expect to have great, ultimate sex on your honeymoon night. Rather, expect to enjoy the process of being naked and not ashamed (Gen. 2:25). Then over the next fifty years of marriage, you can work toward great sex.

Remember, sex is not a seven-minute experience; it is an all-day affair. Thus, perfecting life during those 166 hours a week will help you experience the ultimate in sexual intimacy. The awesome part is God wired us that way.

We do recognize that many people bring baggage and sexual hurts into a marriage. Finding help and healing is important for your marriage. Leader, make sure to connect couples with local Christian counselors or pastors when necessary.

NOTE: *For further discussion about sexual intimacy, consult the Sexual Intimacy Q&A in the appendix of the Bible study book.*

COMMUNICATION *and* CONFLICT MANAGEMENT

CAN WE LEARN TO TALK AND FIGHT EFFECTIVELY FOR OUR MARRIAGE?

OVERVIEW

The purpose of this section is to understand the communication skills involved in managing conflict in your relationship. Communication is the lifeblood of every marriage. Since conflict is inevitable, a married couple needs ways to safely and respectfully work through issues. These principles are key to developing a healthy marriage.

"It takes two to speak the truth—one to speak, and another to hear."[1]

HENRY DAVID THOREAU

KEYS TO LIVING OUT THE VOWS

"Conflict is like water: too much causes damage
to people and property; too little creates a dry,
barren landscape devoid of life and color."[2]
CONSTANTINO AND MERCHANT

SESSION GOAL

To equip couples with tools to learn the necessary skills to effectively communicate by expressing oneself, listening, and managing conflict.

KEY BIBLICAL PRINCIPLES

- Proverbs 15:1; Proverbs 18:13—Listen before responding. A gentle response defuses frustration.
- Matthew 12:34; Proverbs 10:19-20—Words reveal the state of our hearts.
- Luke 6:45—The truth of God stored in our lives will be reflected in our speech.
- Ephesians 4:32—Be kind and compassionate, forgive each other as quickly as Christ forgave us.
- Colossians 4:6—In conversation, bring out the best in others.
- James 1:19—Quick to listen, slow to speak, and slow to become angry.
- James 4:1-6—Pride and selfishness are the main sources of conflict.

Dear Leader,

Communication and conflict resolution are highly predictive of divorce. But good news—they are most amenable to change. It's vital to the success of a marriage that couples understand and apply principles from this section.

As I am sure you can attest to, conflict in marriage is inevitable. Contrary to popular belief, the quality of a marriage is not measured by the number of conflicts or disagreements (or lack thereof) but by the way in which a couple handles conflict when problems arise.

Speaking lovingly and respectfully in the midst of conflict requires great patience and self-control—one more reason why we need a supernatural God to empower us. Help couples realize that it is God's desire to use conflict and problems to perfect our marriage and faith.

Effective, constructive, communication and conflict management is a key component to a happy, healthy, and holy marriage. When you teach couples to fight well, you are instructing them as to how they can fight for their marriage. Marriage is worth fighting for!

"The most basic of all human needs is the need to understand and be understood. The best way to understand people is to listen to them."[3]

RALPH NICHOLS

Is it any wonder that communication is such a tough issue? We all differ in personality and temperament, values and philosophies, background and history. Our attempts to communicate are filtered through these discrepancies. Don't assume that love alone, without skills and understanding, will produce a successful marriage.

Byron and I (Carla) are very aware of how challenging it can be to communicate especially when our differences enter into the conversation. Just recently we had one of those late night conversations where we completely misfired. Actually, it began early in the evening but ended very late in the evening or really early in the morning. We each had our own opinions, and our opinions differed. We were both determined to get our points across. As the discussion progressed and intensified, I slipped into my usual pattern of withdrawing into my "turtle shell." Some people say silence is golden, but in this case, silence was destructive. Byron tends to escalate; so the quieter I got, the more frustrated Byron became.

After a couple of hours of difficult conversation, I realized I needed to consider Byron's point of view. I needed to let go of my pride, truly listen, and seek to understand his heart. Silently avoiding the issue was counterproductive. As we faced the issue, Byron softened his tone; I clearly communicated my thoughts. This allowed Byron to better understand my side of the issue. We had to deny our natural tendencies and focus our efforts on managing the issue. Eventually we worked through our disagreement. Conflict is never fun, but God uses it to whittle away our rough edges, conform us more to His image, and deeply bond us with one another.

BEST PREDICTOR OF FUTURE MARRIAGES

Communicating and managing conflict are the keys to living out your marriage vows. According to psychologists Howard Markman, Scott Stanley, and Susan L. Blumberg, it is not necessarily how much couples love each other that can best predict the future of their relationship but instead how they handle conflict and disagreement.[4]

Markman, Stanley, and Blumberg have carefully researched a sample of one hundred and fifty couples for thirteen years. They observed couples during their engagements and after their wedding days.[5] In their research, using only data collected from couples prior to marriage, they have been able to predict with eighty-two to ninety-three percent accuracy which couples will go on to be divorced and which will stay happily married.[6] This "means . . . for many couples, the seeds of [distress and future] divorce are [planted] prior to marriage."[7] A couple's premarital patterns of communication and conflict resolution may strongly predict divorce. The good news is that conflict management skills are most easily learned and readily produce change.

Since conflict management is highly predictive of divorce and most amenable to change, understanding and applying conflict management expertise is vital to the success of a marriage. Although some things are beyond our control, we can improve in this area. Thus, the challenge is to work hard and continually learn better ways to manage conflict with your (future) spouse.

"All married couples should learn the art of battle as they should learn the art of making love. Good battle is objective and honest— never vicious or cruel. Good battle is healthy and constructive, and brings to a marriage the principle of equal partnership."[8]

ANN LANDERS

How did working through the Bible study book go this week?

STARTER QUESTIONS FROM THE BIBLE STUDY BOOK WILL LEAD INTO THE SESSION.

Does one of you love something the other one hates?

Do you agree on politics? Do you feel a need to agree on all controversial topics like abortion or same-sex marriage? Or are you okay with "agreeing to disagree"?

Which animal did each individual select to best describe the way he or she handles conflict? Why did you choose than animals? (See Prep Work Assignment #3.) Name some of the character qualities you share. What is positive about the way you handle conflict? What is negative?

TRANSITIONAL QUESTION: When growing up, what was your family's pattern of communication? How did they manage conflict?

STATE THE PART OF BIBLICAL PRINCIPLE AND PRESENT THE KEY QUESTION (P. 123) FOR THIS SECTION.

PRAY.

NOTE: *Prior to the session, have couples take the Five-Minute Animal Personality Inventory by Dr. Gary Smalley.[9] Each person completes one on themselves and one for their future mate.*

WHAT IS GOOD COMMUNICATION?

"It seemed rather incongruous that in a society of super-sophisticated communication, we often suffer from a shortage of listeners."[10]

ERMA BOMBECK

Good communication takes place with both partners fully open, authentic, and vulnerable when sharing their ideas, thoughts, and opinions. When partners communicate, they must both feel respected and valued by the other. Good communication skills are basic to any well-functioning relationship and can be learned through practice and commitment. Most difficulties arise when we miscommunicate. When Paul wrote the Colossians, he instructed them on the importance of communicating with grace—instead of the impatience and frustration that are often expressed in the midst of miscommunication: "Let your conversation be always full of grace, seasoned with salt, so that you may know how to answer everyone" (Col. 4:6).

Differences in communication styles are often a result of differing backgrounds, gender, and personalities. These differences may lead to conflict and misunderstanding. All couples bring with them varying backgrounds which strongly influence their communication styles. While some of those characteristics and traits may be helpful in learning to communicate, others may be divisive and damaging to a relationship.

Each partner comes from a family that communicates with particular patterns (both healthy and unhealthy), and couples need to identify those patterns to trace how they have impacted their own ability to communicate.

Differences in communication may also come from gender variation. A relationship benefits from the strengths that each partner brings, and one must be willing to learn the language of his or her partner in order to better communicate. If he is better able to understand with less emotion and drama, then she needs to work to communicate her message in that way. If she understands better with word pictures and examples, then it benefits him to learn to communicate his message in that manner so that she has a greater likelihood to understand.

Personality differences play another vital role in communication.

Think back to the Five-Minute Animal Personality Inventory. A couple may have one partner who is quiet and more passive—often Beavers and Golden Retrievers— while the other is very verbal and extroverted—often Lions and Otters. Each has valuable traits that will prove helpful in learning to communicate. Beavers and Golden Retrievers can help Lions and Otters be better listeners, while the Otters and Lions can help the Golden Retrievers and Beavers find the words to better express themselves.[11]

HOW CAN WE COMMUNICATE EFFECTIVELY?

How often do you sit down as a couple to simply talk with one another? Do you set time aside specifically for this purpose? Why or why not?

Effective listening has the potential to enrich all of our relationships but none more than our marriage relationships. Although speaking comes more easily to some people (Lions and Otters), no communication takes place without someone listening and trying to understand. In Scripture, even James addressed "listening" before "speaking" when he said:

> "Everyone should be quick to listen, slow to
> speak and slow to become angry."
> **JAMES 1:19**

Listening is not a spectator's sport, but it requires active participation. A good listener takes on half of the responsibility for keeping a conversation meaningful and effective. Do you ever feel as if you are talking to a wall? Good listening requires inviting our spouses to share, showing understanding, exploring feelings behind the words, and using reflective listening to clarify what is meant. In reflective listening, you speak back what you understand a person to be saying in an effort to confirm that you correctly understand the message.

Remember, through actively listening to our (future) spouses, we are best able to discern exactly how to communicate effectively when it is our turn to do the speaking.

It is vital that both partners be willing to look at their own patterns of communication and together create a new pattern of communicating—unique to them. Sometimes working through old habits or patterns can be difficult, but developing healthy communication skills is invaluable when seeking the oneness that God intends for a marriage.

"There is an old proverb that says, 'The road to the heart is the ear.' I believe it. That explains why many marriages are growing cold when out of the 10,000 plus minutes in every week, the average couple spends only 17 minutes in close communication. That's a chilling fact."[12]

DAVID L. BROWN

Each partner must accept the responsibility to speak effectively and listen actively:

- It is my responsibility to effectively communicate my message to my partner. If the message is not getting through, I must find another way to communicate it.

- It is my responsibility to understand what my partner is saying. If I am unclear about the message being communicated, I must ask clarifying questions and work to understand what is being communicated.

  Illustration—"20 Phrases to Promote Communication Using Clarifying Questions" (See The Tools, p.143.)

What do you need and expect from each other in terms of openness and depth of communication? How do your needs and expectations differ?

How would you deal with a breach in trust?

BEGINS WITH LISTENING

Most of us are usually slow to listen, quick to speak, and even faster to become angry. As one of our old pastors used to say, "Most of us do not need hearing aids; we just need aid in hearing."

Good listening begins with a complete focus on the one doing the talking. We can be there but not all *there*. Distractions come in many forms.

Being fully present requires active listening. It demands that we reflect on what is being communicated and how it is being said. Often this includes asking the right questions—clarifying what is being said rather than judging or indicting.

LEARNING TO EXPRESS ONESELF

Unsuccessful communication can be similar to speaking in two different languages. If a message were clearly spoken in English to a person who only speaks Spanish, there's a good chance the message would be misunderstood or, at best, only partially understood. A person attempting to communicate a message has the responsibility to speak in a "language" the listener understands. Too often one partner gets angry and frustrated when the other one doesn't comprehend what's being said despite every effort to understand.

We should each determine what we want to say, how we want to say it, and when we want to say it. Using restraint and good judgment when communicating can make a big difference in the effectiveness of a person's message. Proverbs 10:19 (NASB) points out the potential dangers of an uncontrolled tongue:

> "When there are many words, transgression is unavoidable, but he who restrains his lips is wise."

We must remember to consider the listener's background, gender, and personality traits when deciding how to best communicate our message.

What in your communication style (e.g., behavior, tone of voice, choice of words, etc.) might interfere with your (future) spouse's understanding of what you are trying to say?

NEVER ASSUME

We must not assume our partner communicates in the same way we do. For instance, if a husband is passionate about a particular issue, he may simply look his wife in the eyes and calmly but firmly explain his feelings. However, if the wife feels an equal amount of passion, her communication style might look quite different: her tone of voice may become elevated (which he interprets as anger or frustration), she may use what he considers to be wild gestures (often rising to her feet and using hand motions), and she may begin to speak rather rapidly (which he assumes is my way of showing impatience). It is important for him to understand that she is not blowing her top but simply communicating about something for which she feels passionately. Likewise, she must take his message seriously even though he does not display the same kind of communication style that she does.

> *"Being vulnerable doesn't have to be threatening. Just have the courage to be sincere, open, and honest. This opens the door to deeper communication all around. It creates self-empowerment and the kind of connections with others we all want in life."*[13]
>
> **SARA PADDISON**

We should not expect our partners to read between the lines. We have all heard the old axiom, "Say what you mean and mean what you say." We are wrong most of the time when we try to guess what another person is thinking. If we want our spouses to help with the dishes or help clean out the garage, then we need to say just that. You must not expect him or her to read your mind. My husband and I have an agreement: We have decided not to fault each other for not responding to something that was not verbalized. If I do not say it, I cannot expect my spouse to know it.

Spouses need to be careful not to speak rashly, always weighing their words before speaking them. It is also wise to pick an appropriate time and place to speak. You may wake up ready to go into heavy conversation, but your partner, who is not a morning person, may not respond in the way you would like. Avoid words like "should," "ought," and "must." These are considered parenting words and can communicate a sense of arrogance, pride, or superiority. "Always" and "never" may come across as defensive words possibly resulting in a negative response from the listener. They are often not helpful when attempting to communicate a message.

Communicating will eventually become less difficult and miscommunication less frequent as a couple grows, matures, and spends years together. Good communication is the most challenging and difficult during the first years of marriage.

HOW WAS CONFLICT HANDLED IN YOUR HOME OF ORIGIN?

Many of the skills a couple will use in resolving conflict are the same skills needed to communicate effectively. The way a couple deals with conflict is strongly influenced by their backgrounds and personalities. Couples eager to learn how to resolve conflict effectively begin by identifying the origin, root, or pattern from which a problem emanates. Then, they need to choose an approach that works for them, and practice, practice, practice!

A couple must realize that each person has brought some patterns of dealing with conflict into the relationship. (Future) spouses may even have contrasting opinions as to whether or not conflict and differences should be resolved. Unresolved conflict leads to resentment and anger. It has been compared to a deep wound that needs to heal. A person can choose to stitch the wound up, but often that simply traps the infection and can lead to more serious complications in the long run.

Was yelling and screaming a common occurrence in your home? Or was every effort made to avoid conflict and confrontation—even to the detriment of the family?

We all bring baggage into a marriage. Would your baggage fit into a tote bag, suitcase, or a crate? What steps have you taken to "unpack" your baggage?

Does conflict trigger certain emotions in you even today—insecurity, fear, anxiety, anger, etc.?

Emotional wounds need to be healed from the inside out instead of being covered up or buried. The process of resolving conflict can lead to a deeper understanding of one another and greater intimacy as a couple—and there's no better way to exemplify love, mercy, patience, understanding, and faithfulness!

"Difficulties are meant to rouse, not discourage.
The human spirit is to grow strong by conflict."[14]
WILLIAM ELLERY CHANNING

WHAT ARE THE HOT BUTTONS THAT YOUR PARTNER MOST OFTEN PUSHES?

What should you do if you and your (future) spouse come to a situation of conflict and feel strongly that the other person is at fault?

Do you think the level of conflict for most couples will increase or decrease after marriage? Why or why not?

KEY PRINCIPLES IN RESOLVING CONFLICT

- Recognize potential conflict early, before it arises, and especially before it escalates.

- Establish healthy patterns and rules that work and are effective.

- Re-evaluate often. Don't get "stuck in a rut" with patterns or habits that are not effective. Instead, be willing to troubleshoot and try something new.

PROBLEM-SOLVING SKILLS

- Pray first. It is vital to ask God to be part of your discussion since He will be the Author of the solution.

- Take responsibility for your part in the problem instead of blaming your partner.

- Pick your setting, making sure it is an appropriate time and place.

- Pay careful attention to your partner's mind-set and to your own mind-set when introducing a difficult issue.

- Be aware of your tone of voice, body language, and choice of words.

- Identify the problem and stay focused on the solution—not on critiquing each other.

- Keep the discussion current and avoid bringing up past hurts.

- Avoid tangents by maintaining focus on the issue at hand.

- Take a time-out. Agree ahead of time to take a time-out when an argument becomes too heated or frustrating. Agreed upon an amount of time (thirty minutes?), take your break, and then return to the discussion.

- Be willing to compromise: go into the discussion knowing that the goal is not you getting your way.

- Do not air your dirty laundry outside of your marriage, especially to in-laws. You will be able to work through a disagreement and find resolution, but your parents will be much less likely to forgive and forget.

WHAT IS YOUR TYPICAL PATTERN WHEN MANAGING CONFLICT?

Communicating and resolving conflict are the keys to living out the marriage vows. And, as we stated earlier, they can be significant factors in whether a marriage thrives or struggles.

"Peace is not the absence of conflict but the presence of creative alternatives for responding to conflict—alternatives to passive or aggressive responses, alternatives to violence."[15]
DOROTHY THOMPSON

There are four unhealthy patterns that are most common in dealing with conflict.[16] Identify the pattern(s) you tend to exhibit in conflict.

- **Escalation** *"occurs when partners respond back and forth negatively to each other, continually upping the ante so that conditions get worse and worse."[17]*
- **Invalidation** *occurs when "one partner subtly or directly puts down the thoughts, feelings, or character of the other."[18]*
- **Withdrawal** *or* **Avoidance** *occurs when "one partner shows an unwillingness to get into or stay with important discussions. "[19]*
- **Negative Interpretation** *occurs when a person interprets the motives of his or her (future) spouse much more negatively than that person intended.[20]*

What is your typical pattern when managing conflict?

What are you like when you are mad?

What are some positive ways to short-circuit unhealthy patterns of conflict?

HIDER OR HURLER

Hiders are people who struggle with being honest and fail to share their true thoughts and feelings. They are "peace fakers" who say, "No really, everything is fine. I'm fine. Really."

Hurlers are people who are honest and share the truth but in brutal and damaging ways. They are "peace breakers" who say, "You are horrible at managing money! What were you thinking when you bought that?"

Help couples strive to be "peace makers" by working hard to manage their conflict.

CONCLUSION

When two people reach a disagreement, they can choose to fight (both lose) or to problem solve (both win). Each partner must make a conscious choice and decision to attack the problem, instead of attacking each other.

Unlike a fight, when a solution is found through problem-solving, both partners win. When fighting, partners take sides and have a power struggle to see whose argument wins. On the other hand, problem-solving means the partners must work together to exchange ideas, opinions, and suggestions in an effort to reach a compromise or solution. Being kind to each other is never more difficult or necessary than in the midst of a conflict or disagreement.

Thus, the biblical wisdom of Ephesians 4:32 (NASB) proves helpful in any marriage:

> "Be kind to one another, tenderhearted, forgiving each other, just as God in Christ also has forgiven you."

Marriage is worth fighting fair for!

SYNOPSIS

"Men and women have been miscommunicating—or not communicating at all—for thousands of years. And all too often, relationships break down because someone can't 'hear' what his or her spouse is trying to say. All too often, couples give up on a relationship that could have been a success."[21]

HOLLY HUDSON

When I (Carla) slip into my withdrawal pattern and Byron escalates, tensions rise and we completely miss the mark with one another. We have observed that the closest relationships have the highest risk for disappointment, hurt, and rejection. Because of this reality, an important part of good communication is a commitment to forgiveness and resolving conflict. The free exchange of thoughts, ideas, and opinions, engulfed with honesty is also vital to meaningful communication—all the while, couples remaining totally committed to one another.

A FEW KEYS TO SUCCESSFUL COMMUNICATION

As issues arise, we have a choice in how we will respond to these oftentimes painful experiences. My first instinct is to follow my emotional response that may be rooted in selfishness and pride. My second choice is a God-centered, supernatural response rooted in love. Jesus serves as our model.

Good communication requires transparency. For many couples, their families of origin did not model transparency in the home where they were reared. Transparency and vulnerable communication can be difficult, especially for men. As Dr. James Dobson points out, "Research makes it clear that little girls are blessed with greater linguistic ability than little boys, and it remains a lifelong talent. Simply stated, [a wife] talks more than [a husband]. As an adult, she typically expresses her feelings and thoughts far better than her husband and is often irritated by his reticence. God may have given her [fifty thousand] words per day and her husband only [twenty-five thousand]. He comes home from work with 24,975 used up and merely grunts his way through the evening. He may descend into Monday night football while his wife is dying to expend her remaining [twenty-five thousand] words."[22]

God created marriage to be different from all other relationships—one in which we can truly be free to share the deepest parts of ourselves with our spouses. As you think of being transparent with your mate, remember that transparency begins with being open to God. This openness reduces our pride as we humbly trust ourselves to Him. God then gives us the ability to be open with others.

Good communication requires listening. For me to be present with Byron means that I must be prepared to temporarily be absent to myself. More often than not, people speak too much and listen too little—causing communication struggles. Good listening:

- Involves your undivided attention;
- Involves sensitivity and discernment;
- Takes time.

"The pause button on my tongue's remote control should get much more use than the play button."[23]
GARY THOMAS

POWERFUL WORDS HEAL MARITAL HURTS.

Do not bury your hurt feelings, but lovingly confront your mate when you are hurt. Here are some helpful suggestions:

- Have the courage to confront.
- Speak the truth in love (Eph. 4:15).
- Attack the problem and not each other.
- Avoid confronting your mate in public or in front of your children.
- Maintain the humility to confess.

Just as important as confrontation is the need to ask for forgiveness. Three words and three statements are very powerful in healing marital hurts. Three important words—"I was wrong!" lead to three important statements:

- I was wrong.
- I am sorry.
- Please forgive me.

May the Lord grace these couples with courage and humility to practice conflict management. Every day that you are married you will have a chance to build each other up or tear each other down. Your spouse is the greatest gift God has given you—your most prized possession. Use your words to pour courage into your mate. Listen as he or she talks to you. Keep in mind—this is one skill you can actually improve quickly. Remember, the area of communication requires constant attention.

As Byron and I have discovered, learning to communicate and manage conflict is crucial to living out the marriage covenant. This lifelong process will teach you more about yourself and God than you ever thought possible. Hang in there—it is worth the effort!

THE TOOLS

20 PHRASES TO PROMOTE COMMUNICATION USING CLARIFYING QUESTIONS

1. How do you feel about…?
2. What would you like…?
3. What is really good about…?
4. Looks like you're…
5. I sense that…
6. How is it going with…?
7. What's troubling you about…?
8. It sounds like…
9. How do you see…?
10. Say a little more about that…
11. What I hear you saying is…
12. It feels as though…
13. Tell me more about…
14. What happened then?
15. What is the purpose of…?
16. …is that how you see it?
17. Let's check that out with…
18. How do you see the problem with…?
19. Do you see it differently?
20. Can you tell me more about that…?

IN-LAWS
and FUTURE
INTENTIONS

WHERE ARE WE HEADED?

OVERVIEW

The purpose of this section is to help you navigate your homes of origin together as you define healthy patterns for your new marriage. As you evaluate the contents of this study, you will be challenged to think through, dream about, and pray for your future together as husband and wife.

> *"A journey is like marriage. The certain way to be wrong is to think you control it."* [1]
>
> **JOHN STEINBECK**

> # "A MAN WILL LEAVE HIS FATHER AND MOTHER AND CLEAVE UNTO HIS WIFE."

"If you cannot get rid of the family skeleton,
you may as well make it dance."[2]
GEORGE BERNARD SHAW

SESSION GOAL

To discuss family history and ascertain proper expectations as the couple begins a new path together—creating their own traditions, memories, and rich experiences, all the while, navigating healthy patterns that "honor father and mother," siblings, and previous family traditions. To reflect on all of the past Bible study book sections and set a course of action for the married life ahead.

KEY BIBLICAL PRINCIPLES

- Exodus 18:13-24—God uses parents and in-laws to offer sage advice.
- Exodus 20:12; Ephesians 6:2-3—Honor parents.
- Psalm 78:1-8—Leave a legacy.
- Proverbs 29:18—Vision and intentionality give life.
- Ephesians 5:31-33—Move beyond parental dependence to create a new family.

Dear Leader,

Your journey with the couple(s) has come to an end. Thank you for your investment of time, energy, love, and grace.

It would be really easy for couples to run toward the wedding and on to a new marriage without ever slowing down to acknowledge the path they have journeyed.

This final session is designed to slow these couples down enough to reflect on all of your past sessions and discussions. Then, we'll challenge them to create future intentions for their new family unit as they leave father and mother.

Don't forget to celebrate the couple's completion of To Have and To Hold. It is impressive for a couple to put in the more than twenty hours of time in preparation for marriage. Please commit to pray for them in the days ahead.

As each couple stands at the altar and states their vows, they are now better prepared to live them out as they give a correct portrayal of our holy God and enjoy marriage in the process. Join us in praying for each couple to leave a godly legacy.

Thank you for pouring into future marriages. Our hope is for biblical principles to be passed on from this generation to the next. May God bless you for the time and energy you've invested into future marriages.

The best is yet to come! Thank you for leaving a legacy.

These days, we have a tendency to move from one event to the next. Our lifestyles are not conducive to reflection or using mementos to remind us of particular experiences. The engagement period and first years of marriage are a good time of assessment. It's really easy to run past the wedding and into a new marriage without slowing down to evaluate life and provide intentional direction for the future.

When you marry, people say, you don't just marry your partner, you marry two families. Which is true. You're not just entering into a relationship with your spouse; you're entering into ongoing, lifelong relationships with your in-laws as well.

But it's also true that as you cleave to your mate, you are leaving your family of origin. When you marry, you create a new family of your own—a separate spiritual unit. It's the *two* that become one. Not the six. Not the eleven.

EXTENSIVE TRANSITION

For some of you, leaving your past family history and marrying into a fresh start is a very welcome change. However, if you fail to learn from your struggles and heal past hurts, it will be difficult to enter into a healthy marriage relationship. Every marriage will undoubtedly have struggles of its own. For others of you, leaving home will be the toughest part of getting married because you have a favorable family past with many rich traditions and warm memories.

"If you want to go quickly, go alone. If you want to go far, go together."[3]
AFRICAN PROVERB

Hopefully during these weeks of learning how "to have and to hold" one another in your new marriage, you have gained a few new skills and have encountered God in a real and personal way. To live intentionally, it is crucial to put into practice all that you are learning. Leaving and cleaving requires gaining a vision of where you are headed. Proverbs 29:18 (KJV) reminds us, "Where there is no vision the people perish."

Simply put, leaving and cleaving involves an extensive transition, and it is vital for you to reflect on the past while walking into the future.

How did working through the Bible study book go this week?

STARTER QUESTIONS FROM THE BIBLE STUDY BOOK WILL LEAD INTO THE SESSION.

What three words best describe your relationship with your father? Your mother? Are you afraid of becoming like your mom? Dad? Why or why not?

On a scale of one (distant and unconnected) to ten (very strong connection), how connected are you to your parents? Do you foresee any potential issues for your (future) spouse regarding your relationship with your parents?

What is one thing you would like to take from your home of origin? What is one thing you hope to leave behind?

TRANSITIONAL QUESTION: What dreams do you have for your marriage? How are you going to pursue godly goals as you move forward toward a healthy, lasting relationship?

STATE THE PART OF THE BIBLICAL PRINCIPLE AND PRESENT THE KEY QUESTION (P. 145) FOR THIS SECTION.

PRAY.

HOW DO YOU CREATE A NEW FAMILY UNIT?

HELPFUL TIP: *It is beneficial to be authentic and honest about your in-law struggles. However, remember the session is about the couple(s)—not you.*

People say it all the time, "You don't just marry your partner, you marry two families." Which is true. Couples are entering into ongoing, lifelong relationships with in-laws.

Simply put, leaving and cleaving involves an extensive transition. It is vital for couples to reflect on the past while walking into the future.

Basically understood, oneness in marriage is in alignment and agreement with God's will and purpose.

What is the purpose of your new marriage?

What kind of marriage partners do we want to be? How do we want to treat each other?

What kind of parents would we want to be? What principles would we want to teach our children to help them prepare for adulthood and to lead responsible, caring lives?

MORE THAN MOVING OUT

"Leaving father and mother" involves far more than just moving out of the house. It means moving beyond full dependence upon them. When dependency continues, it is often due to one or both parties refusing to detach. This may be due to a variety of issues. To maintain a healthy long-term relationship, separation must take place.

Sociologists have identified two factors as being highly significant to the success of a marriage: 1) whether people have emotionally separated from their parents in a healthy way and 2) whether they have had an opportunity to live on their own, by themselves, before they are married. If both of these conditions existed, individuals have a better opportunity for a successful marriage.[4]

DOES HONORING PARENTS AND OBEYING THEM GO HAND IN HAND?

It is very important that newly married couples work toward a healthy relationship by loving and honoring their parents.

When parents are actively involved in their children's lives, of course, they'll probably have relational capital to offer their opinions. Unfortunately many parents today are either not very involved or are over-involved in their children's lives. As we grow into adults, we increasingly come to see that everyone, including our parents, has baggage. Unfortunately, parents' baggage—controlling behavior, unreasonable expectations for their children, and immature actions—can sometimes surface during the engagement period. Put bluntly, some parents can even be less mature than their own children.

If there are struggles, tension, or past hurts, encourage the couple to have an honest conversation with their parents about disagreements or past baggage. Perhaps encourage them to write a letter to open a dialogue.

In Paul's letter to the Ephesians, he begins the chapter by telling children to "obey your parents in the Lord, for this is right" (Eph. 6:1). That word *obey* is said "of one who on a knock at the door comes to listen who it is."[5] Paul continues by quoting the Old Testament book of Exodus, "'Honor your father and mother'—which is the first commandment with a promise—'so that it may go well with you and that you may enjoy long life on this earth'" (Eph. 6:2-3; Ex. 20:12). Part of getting married is becoming an adult—children don't get married. Children need discipline and structure from a parent. Adults need self-discipline. Yet, both children and adults must continue to honor their fathers and mothers.

> *Is it okay for either of you to talk with parents about the problems in your marital relationship?*

AVOID TRIANGULATION

Point out that sometimes cultural expectations differ between a newly married couple and their parents. Parents may not think the couple is old enough to get married. Parents may have their own prejudices regarding a partner's socio-economic level or education—or they may have outright racial prejudices. Whatever the issue—no matter how much a couple disagrees with their parents' views, their prejudice, perhaps even their hatred—it is important to strive to honor father and mother. We have seen how difficult this can be among the couples we know.

When conflict does occur, avoid triangulation: when three parties are involved in a he said/she said disagreement. Usually one says something about the other to a third party instead of going directly to the other person.

It is important to sit down and talk respectfully face-to-face with the involved party about what you sense coming between you. Always have a united front as a couple, and allow the son or daughter to deal directly with his or her parent. The key is to show respect—regardless of how the parents respond. Couples are creating a new legacy of their own.

What expectations do you have for being together with your extended family? How much is too much connectedness for you?

What kind of support do you expect from your partner his or her the parents are putting pressure on you?

ESTABLISHING HEALTHY BOUNDARIES

When a father rejects his daughter's fiancé because the man doesn't meet the father's expectations, he probably isn't thinking much about how his actions might impact his relationship with both of them. When a mother leaves a father for another man, she probably isn't thinking about the full consequences of her actions in the years to come. When a father abuses alcohol and loses control of himself, he probably isn't thinking down the road to being unwelcome at his son's wedding. It would be easy to respond vindictively to any pain that has been dealt.

Strive to resist returning the favor in the face of a trying relationship. It is a test of love and we aren't saying it's easy to love in such situations. But then, God never said love would be easy.

It is important for couples to set healthy, appropriate boundaries so that they aren't continually hurt. As you strive to honor your parents, remember you can't change them or their responses. The only thing you can change is your response. As our good friend, Jim Wimberly, has told his children for years, "You are only responsible for your responses."

What can be learned from Exodus 20:12 and Ephesians 6:2-3?

How is honoring and respecting our parents obeying the Lord? Does this mean we must follow all of their advice? Why? Why not?

Illustration—"In-Law Panel Discussion" (See The Tools, p.160.)

WHO GIVES THIS BRIDE AWAY?

The symbolism of the father giving the bride away at the altar provides a beautiful picture of what it means to leave and to cleave. In biblical times, a young man had to earn his right to marry the bride. Although both the groom's father and the bride's father determined the arrangement, it was not uncommon for a young man to be required to work for years to pay a dowry for his new bride. This was not considered a payment or a purchase price for a wife but was compensation to the father for the loss of her help as a daughter.

For parents, marriage is a bittersweet time. It is especially confusing for them because they are trying to let go while at the same time hanging on to a close relationship with their child. It is best, at the altar and in life, for the parents to give their blessings and then move to the background to offer support.

Certainly, families are still very important; but, parents are no longer the key people in the bride and groom's lives.

The word *leave* in Genesis 2:24 implies "to loosen," "relinquish," or "permit."[6] Thus, parents must loosen their grip, relinquish control, and allow their child to move forward, all the while offering support.

The portion of the ceremony where the bride is given to the groom is significant because it is a statement from the most important man in the bride's life to her new groom. Her father is, in effect, saying, "I have loved, provided, and protected my valued possession up until this point—now I am entrusting her to you. Take good care of her." Or in cases where a father is not present, family and friends stand with the bride and give her away, charging the new husband with the care and responsibility of the family unit being created, including the bride's spiritual, emotional, and physical well-being.

It is the responsibility of the couple to create a new path together while creating their own traditions, warm memories, and rich experiences. Each must remember that his or her spouse is now the first priority.

As a couple strives to honor their parents, remember Paul's admonition in Ephesians 5 to be imitators of Christ and "live a life of love, just as Christ loved us" (NCV).

HOW DO VISION AND INTENTIONALITY PROVIDE MEANING FOR LIFE?

Gaining vision compels us to gather information. There is no better time than just before or immediately after a wedding to create future intentions. At this point in the couple's marriage preparation, instruct them to reflect back over *all* of your past sessions and discuss a vision for their married life. During the process, each couple should evaluate:

• Who are they, individually and as a couple?

• Where do they come from (emotionally, spiritually, physically)?

• What kind of support system do they have in place?

   How is creating a family mission statement valuable to our future intentions?

How can we both support each other in our respective goals?

How do we want to give back?

How do we imagine our marriage ten years from now?

Revisit Prep Work #4 with the couple(s), prompting them to think through their future intentions and a family mission statement. Proverbs 29:18 (KJV) says, "Where there is no vision, the people perish." Vision and intentionality give life to newly married couples.

"What would be worse than being born blind?
To have sight without vision." [7]
HELEN KELLER

WHAT LEGACY WILL YOU LEAVE?

PILING UP STONES

After an encounter with God, Old Testament characters would often build an altar or rename a place as a reminder to everyone of God's providence. Instead of rapidly moving from event to event and never looking back, these men knew how to stop and celebrate God's visit. We can learn a great lesson from these faithful men and women. Sometimes we need to slow down enough to reflect on all that God has done in our lives, evaluate, and eagerly move forward. We need to pile up some stones as we celebrate God's activity in our lives.

As you look back, tradition, conflict, and great memories have made you who you are. We cannot escape the past, but we must value and appreciate where we have been. Evaluating life helps us to pass on a righteous legacy to the next generation.

The Bible says in Psalm 78:

> "Things we have heard and known, things our ancestors
> have told us. We will not hide them from their descendants;
> we will tell the next generation the praiseworthy deeds of
> the Lord, his power, and the wonders he has done."
> **PSALM 78:3-4**

It is crucial to put into practice all that we have learned. Leaving and cleaving requires gaining a vision of where we are headed.

What do we want to be known for? What reputation do we want to have? What is the key theme you would want to hear at your funeral or the words you'd want etched on your tombstone?

What does success look like for our new family?

What do we want to pass on to the next generation? How will we go about doing this?

How can our marriage best represent the values we believe?

CONCLUSION: THE JOURNEY AHEAD

As couples travel down the path of life, they will need a guide and counselor to make the dreams of this marriage work. Jesus promised in John 14 to send a Counselor, the Holy Spirit, who would be ever-present in our lives. Scripture also tells us that believers in Christ will bear much fruit, and Galatians 5:22-23 (NASB) defines that fruit of the Spirit as love, joy, peace, patience, kindness, goodness, faithfulness, gentleness, and self-control. 1 Corinthians 13 reads:

"Love is patient, love is kind. It does not envy, it does not boast,
it is not proud. It does not dishonor others, it is not self-seeking,
it is not easily angered, it keeps no record of wrongs. Love does
not delight in evil but rejoices with the truth. It always protects,
always trusts, always hopes, always perseveres. Love never fails."
1 CORINTHIANS 13:4-8

We need love to survive and a holy God to empower us to love like He loves.

Challenge couples to cooperate with God's Spirit in their lives—to seek God and His understanding as we journey down the trail. Hang on! Life is full of adventure, and the best part is that God faithfully provides.

"For the LORD gives wisdom; from his mouth
come knowledge and understanding."
PROVERBS 2:6

"By wisdom a house is built, and through understanding
it is established; through knowledge its rooms are
filled with rare and beautiful treasures."
PROVERBS 24:3-4

As they meet at the altar, may their wedding days fulfill the couples' dreams. But, more importantly, challenge them to allow the Holy Spirit to help them fulfill their marriage vows. Keep in mind:

"Though one may be overpowered, two can defend
themselves. A cord of three strands is not quickly broken."
ECCLESIASTES 4:12

HELPFUL TIP: *Celebrate the conclusion of this course by providing a "memorial marker," a stone or a picture, to remind the couple of all they have experienced in preparing for marriage.*

SYNOPSIS

MORE THAN MOVING OUT

"Leaving father and mother" involves far more than just moving out of the house. It means moving beyond full dependence upon them. This requires leaving a parent-centered life and a parent-controlled life where your emotions and decisions revolve around your parents. Again, note two of the factors sociologists have identified as being highly significant to the success of a marriage are:

1. Whether people have emotionally separated from their parents in a healthy way;

2. Whether people have had an opportunity to live on their own, by themselves, before they married.

If both of these conditions exist, individuals have a better opportunity for a successful marriage.[8]

HONOR THY FATHER AND MOTHER

Whether you have a close relationship with your parents now or not, work toward a healthy relationship by loving and honoring your parents. As we grow into adults, we increasingly realize that everyone, including our parents, has baggage. We all need grace and forgiveness.

It is important to avoid triangulation—when three parties are involved in a he said/she said disagreement and one says something about the other to a third party instead of going directly to the person. Couples should have a united front and allow the son or daughter to deal directly with his or her parent. The key is to show honor and respect. Open and honest communication is vital.

WHO GIVES THIS BRIDE AWAY?

The symbolism of the father giving the bride away at the altar provides a beautiful picture of what it means to leave and to cleave. In biblical times, a young man had to earn his right to marry the bride. Although both the groom's father and the bride's father determined the arrangement, it was not uncommon for a young man to be required to work for years to pay a dowry to compensate for the loss of a daughter's help to the family.

When I (Byron) gave our daughter away at the altar, I realized that it is a significant statement from the most important man in the bride's life to her new groom. A father is, in effect, saying, "I've loved, provided, and protected my valued possession up until this point—now I am entrusting her to you. Take good care of her." Or in cases where a father is not present, family and friends stand with the bride and give her away, charging the new husband with the care and responsibility of the family unit being created—including the bride's spiritual, emotional, and physical well-being.

Certainly, families are still very important, but parents are no longer the key people in the bride and groom's life. At the altar and in life, parents must loosen their grip, relinquish control, and offer support as they give their blessing. Then, they should take a 50-yard-line seat to be the biggest fans.

THE JOURNEY AHEAD—CREATING A LEGACY

The couple is the responsible to create a new path together all the while creating their own traditions, warm memories, and rich experiences. The framework you lay today will guide, stretch, and determine the direction of your marriage.

Remember, the first five years of marriage may either lay a foundation you can build on or they may cause you to spend the next five to ten years trying to dig out of the rubble.

During the engagement and marriage process it is vital to evaluate who you are, where you have come from, and what kind of support system you have in place.

As you meet at the altar, may your wedding day fulfill your dreams. More importantly, we challenge you to cooperate with God's Spirit in your life as you learn to love like He loves. As you journey down the trail, hang on! It is full of adventure, and the best part is that God faithfully works and provides in our lives (Phil. 1:6).

> "By wisdom a house is built, and through understanding
> it is established; through knowledge its rooms are
> filled with rare and beautiful treasures."
> **PROVERBS 24:3-4**

> "For the LORD gives wisdom, and from his mouth
> come knowledge and understanding."
> **PROVERBS 2:6**

By the way, don't forget to enjoy the process. Have fun! The best is yet to come.

THE TOOLS

IN-LAW PANEL DISCUSSION

Find three to six married couples to sit on the panel. It is helpful to have a newly married couple (married less than five years), a couple married ten to twenty years, and a couple married more than twenty-five years on the panel. Allow engaged couples to text questions to a moderator or write questions on 3-by-5 index cards.

Poll Everywhere (polleverywhere.com) is a helpful tool. It's an audience response system that uses mobile phones. It will allow couples to anonymously ask questions and display them on a monitor for all participants to see.

Here are some potential questions to get you started:

IN-LAW DISCUSSION QUESTIONS

1. What should we do when one of the parents disapproves of the marriage?

2. How do you deal with a simple conflict of opinion between a spouse and a parent?

3. How do you handle controlling parents or in-laws?

4. How much should you talk about marital struggles with your in-laws?

5. How should you approach a problem you are experiencing with your spouse's parents?

6. Both parents and step parents live in the same city. How do you balance time between them?

7. My mother-in-law thinks her son is perfect and can do no wrong. *Help!*

8. Do in-laws or parents back off from trying to be such a huge part of your life once you're married?

9. I have lots of competition with my fiancé's family for his attention and time. How should I respond in situations like this?

10. What do you do when a parent is overly clingy to your future spouse?

11. My mom is constantly trying to make sure we like her and my family more than my sweetie's. How can I make her understand that I don't want to play favorites?

12. Why is my fianceé so close to her mom? They talk about everything!

13. What are you supposed to do when both families give advice on how to handle finances, child raising, where to live etc.?

14. Is my spouse going to look like her parents?

15. I don't feel like his mother accepts me. How can I talk to him about this?

16. What should I do if my future mother-in-law always wants the spotlight?

17. How do you handle big financial gifts from parents?

18. How much do you involve in-laws in big financial decisions?

19. Does it get worse—in-laws trying to be part of everything – when we have kids?

20. How do we choose whose family to be with on holidays?

21. Do women tend to want to see their family more often? Or men? Who tends to do more of the compromising?

22. What advice can you give me in dealing with supersensitive in-laws?

23. How would you deal with two sets of in-laws? We don't want to always be worrying about "time sharing" and being completely equal. Can you encourage us not to worry?

24. My fiancé's mother is single. How do I tell her that I will be the most important women in my husband's life and he won't be her surrogate husband?

25. If you spend the night at the in-laws' house, is it okay to have sex?

FIGURE 1

CONSENT TO PREMARITAL EDUCATION

OUR GOAL—Our goal in providing marriage preparation is to help you meet the challenges of life in a way that will please and honor the Lord Jesus Christ and allow you to fully enjoy His love for you and His plans for your life.

BIBLICAL BASIS—We believe that the Bible provides thorough guidance and instruction for faith and life. Therefore, our counseling is based on scriptural principles rather than upon those of secular psychology or psychiatry. The leaders of this ministry/study are not trained or licensed as psychotherapists or mental health professionals, nor should they be expected to follow the methods of such specialists.

NOT PROFESSIONAL ADVICE—Some of our leaders work in professional fields outside the church. When serving as leaders within this ministry/study, however, they do not provide the same kind of professional advice and services that they do when they are hired in their professional capacities. Therefore, if you have significant legal, financial, medical, or other technical questions, you should seek advice from an independent professional. Our leaders will be happy to cooperate with such advisors and help you to consider their counsel in the light of relevant scriptural principles.

CONFIDENTIALITY—Confidentiality is an important aspect of the premarital counseling process, and we will carefully guard the information you entrust to us. There are four situations, however, when it may be necessary for us to share certain information with others: 1) When a leader is uncertain as to how to address a particular problem and needs to seek advice from another pastor in the church; 2) When a counselee attends another church and it is necessary to talk with his or her pastor; 3) When there is a clear indication that someone may be harmed unless others intervene; or 4) When a person persistently refuses to renounce a particular sin and it becomes necessary to seek the assistance of others in the church to encourage repentance and reconciliation (see Prov. 15:22; 24:11; Matt. 18:15-20). Please be assured that our leaders strongly prefer not to disclose personal information to others, and they will make every effort to help you find ways to resolve a problem as privately as possible.

RESOLUTION OF CONFLICTS—On rare occasions, a conflict may develop between a leader and a participant. In order to make sure that any such conflicts will be resolved in a biblically faithful manner, we require all of our participants to agree that any dispute that arises with a leader or with this ministry/study as a result of premarital counseling will be settled by mediation and, if necessary, legally binding arbitration in accordance with the *Rules of Procedure* of the Institute for Christian Conciliation. Judgment upon an arbitration award may be entered in any court having jurisdiction.

Having clarified the principles and policies of our ministry/study, we welcome the opportunity to minister to you in the name of Christ and to be used by Him as He helps you to grow in spiritual maturity and prepares you for usefulness in His body. If you have any questions about these guidelines, please contact

_____ of _____.

Please sign below to acknowledge your consent to premarital education.

His Signature: _____ Date: _____

Her Signature: _____ Date: _____

FIGURE 2

CLERGY AND/OR
COUNSELOR PERMISSION

We give permission to _____, if so requested, to send

our _____ results to:
　　　　　(Name of study/test)

_____ The clergy who will perform the wedding ceremony

_____ Our private counselor or therapist

Signed: _____ and _____

Date: _____

OPTIONAL INTRODUCTORY MEETING:

MEET & GREET

This first meeting outline would be useful in a small group or retreat setting. This optional introductory meeting would occur before Session 1.

OVERVIEW

The purpose of the first meeting together is to build relationships, establish trust, and set the road map for your journey together. Remember to have fun, laugh, and help each couple feel at ease. In addition, it is important to allow time for each couple to tell their story.

"Let us always meet each other with a smile, for the smile is the beginning of love."[1]

MOTHER TERESA

SESSION GOAL

To build relationships, establish trust, and set the road map for your journey together

SUPPLIES

- *Please provide each participant with a name tag.*
- *Markers and paper—Have one marker per couple and three to four sheets of blank paper for the NearlyWed game.*

GETTING TO KNOW ONE ANOTHER

At this first session provide snacks and beverages, etc. People need something "to hide" behind. Thus, most of us feel more comfortable eating or drinking something in a new social setting.

Upon arrival, give a quick introduction to the Bible study book, and describe the rhythm of working through each session. The *To Have and To Hold* Bible study book is designed for couples to first attend the introductory session and then follow up, working through the "Intro" and the "Prep Work" of the next session. Then, at the next meeting, the "Driving Questions" will guide your conversation. Note: the participants have plenty of white space to take notes or jot down other questions. Each session concludes with the "Synopsis" which reinforces the content of the session. This rhythm will be repeated for every session until completion.

HELPFUL TIP: *When the leader separates the group, do not tell the men what the women are doing and vice versa.*

---

1. SEPARATE MEN AND WOMEN.

- *Women: The NearlyWed Game (See The Tools, p.169.)*
- *Men: A Guy Thing (See The Tools, p.169.)*

2. BRING COUPLES BACK TOGETHER.

3. PLAY THE NEARLYWED GAME.

4. ALLOW COUPLE(S) TO TELL THEIR STORIES.

- *Guy: How did you first meet?*
- *Girls: How did he propose to you?*

5. GIVE A BRIEF BIBLICAL OVERVIEW:

Marriage is one of the most rewarding, yet difficult, types of relationships. Thank the couple(s) for making the investment to work through *To Have and To Hold.*

Leader, begin with God, "in the beginning"—chapters one and two in Genesis. As God created the land, water, animals, etc., He saw that "it was good." He then created man, and saw that "it was good." However, in Genesis 2:18, He says, "It is not good." God goes on to say that man is not to be alone. Out of man's aloneness, a helper and companion was created. A couple can expect companionship in marriage (more on this subject in later sections).

Marriage gives us the big picture of God's love. We need to communicate to couples that marriage is God's design to demonstrate Himself to us and to show us how to give and receive love. This involves an open, honest, vulnerable, and emotional love. Out of this love comes the ability for a man and woman within the covenant of marriage to "multiply; fill the earth" (Gen. 1:28, NKJV).

THREE REASONS GOD INSTITUTED MARRIAGE
1. Companionship: "not good to be alone" (Gen. 2:18)

2. Intimacy: "one flesh" sexual/emotional/vulnerability (Gen. 2:24)

3. Procreation: "multiply; fill the earth" (Gen. 1:28, NKJV)

More than any other relationship, marriage will expose our hearts and demand growth.

Leader, as you begin this journey with couple(s), please challenge them to think through their expectations and God's reason for the institution of marriage. In the days ahead, marriage will challenge them in ways a couple could never imagine. Marriage is part of the growth process (sanctification) of life, and each of us should learn to love so others can see the kingdom of God at work. The rewards of married life are worth working for.

AS YOU CONCLUDE, PLEASE PRAY FOR EACH COUPLE.

THE TOOLS

WOMEN—NEARLYWED GAME
(like the NewlyWed game show on TV)

USE A FEW OF THE FOLLOWING QUESTIONS, AND CREATE YOUR OWN.

He spares no expense when it comes to _____, and
He is rather cheap when it comes to _____.
When/Where was your first kiss?
Do you put the toilet paper on the holder with the edge over or under?

MEN—A GUY THING

LEADER, PLEASE TAKE THE MEN INTO A DIFFERENT ROOM. GIVE THEM TWO ASSIGNMENTS, AND THEN LEAVE THEM IN THE ROOM ALONE.

HELPFUL TIP: *The men's leader leaving the room forces the future husbands to interact and not be dependent on the leader. A leader will emerge among the future grooms and help bring the group together. Although they will be uncomfortable, this will help thrust them into better communication and relating to one another.*

ASSIGNMENTS:

1. Tell the men to learn each other's first names.

2. They must create a list of Top Five Most Ridiculous Things a Groom Has to Do in the Engagement.

ENDNOTES

CREATING AN EXPERIENCE

1. C. Silvester Home, *David Livingston: Man of Prayer and Action* (Arlington Heights, IL: Christian Liberty Press, 1999), iii.

2. Kathryn Vasel, "Couples Are Spending A Record Amount to Get Married" *CNN Money*, February 2, 2017, accessed on March 13, 2017. Available online at *money.cnn.com/2017/02/02/pf/cost-of-wedding-budget-2016-the-knot*.

3. Maggie Seaver, "The National Average Cost of a Wedding Hits $35, 329" *The Knot* accessed on March 13, 2017. Available online at written *theknot.com/content/average-wedding-cost-2016*.

SESSION 1

1. Stephen M. Crotts, "The Ties that Bind" *Carolina Study Center*, accessed on March 15, 2017. Available online at *carolinastudycenter.com/the-ties-that-bind*.

2. David Boehi, Brent Nelson, Jeff Schulte, and Lloyd Shadrach, Dennis Rainey, ed., *Preparing for Marriage* (Bloomington, Minnesota: Bethany House Publishers, 1998).

3. Paul Tsika, Billie Kaye Tsika, *Get Married, Stay Married* (Shippensburg, PA: Destiny Image® Publishers, Inc., 2010).

4. Gifty Agyemang, *Family Bonding* (Bloomington, IN: AuthorHouse™ UK, 2015).

5. James Strong, *Strong's Exhaustive Concordance of the Bible*, accessed on March 13, 2017, via Bible Hub. Available online at *biblehub.com/hebrew/1285.htm*.

6. Jason D. Scott, *The Strength to Walk Away* (McKinney, TX: Integrity Oasis Publishing, LLC, 2016).

7. H. Norman Wright, *The Secrets of a Lasting Marriage* (Ventura, CA: Gospel Light, 1995), accessed via *mywsb.com*.

8. Gary Smalley and John Trent, *Love Is a Decision: Proven Techniques to Keep Your Marriage Alive and Lively* (Nashville: Thomas Nelson, 1989).

9. Dr. James Dobson, "Q & A–Practical Suggestions for Selecting a Husband" *Dobson Digital Library* Accessed on March 17, 2017. Available online at *dobsonlibrary.com/resource/article/13d44e07-aec7-47ef-9eb5-23f319d646f4*.

10. Tony Evans, *Marriage Matters* (Chicago: Moody Publishers, 2010).

11. David Egner, *What is the promise of marriage?* (Grand Rapids: RBC Ministries, 1992), 6.

12. David Boehi, Brent Nelson, Jeff Schulte, and Lloyd Shadrach, Dennis Rainey, Ed., *Preparing for Marriage* (Bloomington, MN: Bethany House, 1998).

13. Ibid.

14. Ibid.

SESSION 2

1. H. Norman Wright, *Starting Out Together: A Devotional for Dating or Engaged Couples* (Bloomington, Minnesota: Bethany House Publishers, 1996).

2. Frank E. Gaebelein, ed., *The Expositor's Bible Commentary: Volume 11* (Grand Rapids: Zondervan, 1981), accessed via *mywsb.com*.

3. Ibid.

4. John MacArthur, *The MacArthur New Testament Commentary: Ephesians* (Chicago: The Moody Bible Institute of Chicago, 1986), accessed via *mywsb.com*.

5. James Strong, *Strong's Exhaustive Concordance of the Bible*, accessed on March 15, 2017, via Blue Letter Bible. Available online at *blueletterbible.org/lang/lexicon/lexicon.cfm?strongs=G2776*.

6. Matthew George Easton, *Easton's Illustrated Bible Dictionary* (New York: Cosimos, Inc., 2005), accessed via *mywsb.com*.

7. Robert Lewis and William Hendricks, *Rocking the Roles: Building a Win-Win Marriage* (Colorado Springs: NavPress 1991).

8. Ibid, Strong.

9. Constable, Thomas. DD., "Commentary on Ephesians 5:4." *The Expository Notes of Dr. Thomas Constable. Study Light.* Accessed on April 25, 2017. Available online at *studylight.org/commentaries/dcc/ephesians-5.html14?print=yes.*

10. Ibid, Strong, "`ezer."

11. Ibid, Strong, "neged."

12. Ibid, Strong, "nagad."

13. Ibid, Strong, "definition of head."

14. Ibid, Strong, Genesis 2:18.

15. Ibid, Strong, "to aid or help."

16. Ibid, Strong, "Counterpart."

17. Gary L. Thomas, *Sacred Influence: How God Uses Wives to Shape the Souls of Their Husbands* (Grand Rapids: Zondervan, 2006).

18. Brogan Driscoll, "1950s Marriage Advice For Women Will Make Your Feminist Blood Boil" *Huffpost UK Women* August 12, 2016, accessed on March 15, 2017. Available online at *huffingtonpost.co.uk/entry/1950s-marriage-advice_uk_58492e93e4b05b849b67e344.*

SESSION 3

1. Dave Ramsey, *The Total Money Makeover: Proven Plan for Financial Fitness* (Nashville: Thomas Nelson, 2003), 30.

2. Ron Blue, *Master Your Money: A Step-by-Step Plan for Experiencing Financial Contentment* (Chicago: Moody Publishers, 1986).

3. Warren W. Wiersbe, *The Wiersbe Bible Commentary: Old Testament* (Colorado Springs: David C. Cook, 2007), 1081.

4. Erin El Issa, "2016 American Household Credit Card Debt Study" *Nerdwallet blog* Accessed on March 15, 2017. Available online at *nerdwallet.com/blog/average-credit-card-debt-household.*

5. Kate Gibson, "Who lives paycheck-to-paycheck? You might be surprised." *CBS News Moneywatch* August 11, 2016, accessed on March 15, 2017. Available online at *cbsnews.com/news/who-lives-paycheck-to-paycheck-you-might-be-surprised.*

6. Lisa L. Payne, Kim Olver, and Deborah Roth, "The 10 Most Common Reasons People Get Divorced" *The Huffington Post Blog* September 16, 2015, accessed on March 17, 2017. Available online at *huffingtonpost.com/yourtango/10-most-common-reasons-people-divorce_b_8086312.html.*

7. Crown Financial, "The Financial Message of the Ministry" *Crown.org* January 25, 2012, accessed on March 15, 2017. Available online at *crown.org/Articles/tabid/107/entryid/83/Default.aspx.*

8. Adapted from Crown Financial Ministries, "Budget Busters, Part 1 and 2" *Focus on the Family* 2007, accessed on March 17, 2017. Available online at *focusonthefamily.com/lifechallenges/managing-money/battling-the-monthly-budget/budget-busters-part-1* and *focusonthefamily.com/lifechallenges/managing-money/battling-the-monthly-budget/budget-busters-part-2.*

9. Adapted from "10 Things You Can Do To Find Financial Freedom" *Church Alive!* 2011, accessed on March 17, 2017. Available online at *churchaliveabq.com/10thingsyoucandotofindfinancialfreedom.*

SESSION 4

1. Jill Savage, "Seven Ways to Develop Emotional Intimacy in Your Marriage" *Crosswalk.com* December 10, 2010, accessed on March 14, 2017. Available online at *crosswalk.com/family/marriage/seven-ways-to-develop-emotional-intimacy-in-your-marriage-11642928.html.*

2. Gary Thomas, "How to build a lifelong love: an interview with Gary Thomas" *Focus on the Family Canada* 2016, accessed on March 15, 2017. Available online at *focusonthefamily.ca/marriage/communication/how-to-build-a-lifelong-love-an-interview-with-gary-thomas.*

3. Meg Selig, "Know Yourself? 6 Specific Ways to Know Who You Are" *Psychology Today blog* March 9, 2016, accessed on May

5, 2017. Available online at *psychologytoday. com/blog/changepower/201603/know-your- self-6-specific-ways-know-who-you-are.*

4. James Dobson, "Twelve Marriage Killers" *Dr. James Dobson's Family Talk™* accessed on March 17, 2017. Available online at *drjamesdobson.org/articles/ voice-you-trust/12_marriage_killers.*

5. David Hawkins, "Sexual Intimacy Begins with the Heart" Crosswalk.com June 21, 2011 accessed on May 3, 2017. Available online at *crosswalk.com/family/marriage/ doctor-david/sexual-intimacy-begins-with- the-heart-11628157.html.*

6. David and Teresa Ferguson, *Intimate Encoun- ters* (Austin: Intimacy Press, 1997), 10.

7. "Definition of Honor" *Merriam-Webster's Dictionary* accessed on March 17, 2017. Available online at *merriam-webster.com/ dictionary/honor.*

8. "Definition of Honor" *Merriam-Websters' Learner's Dictionary* accessed on March 17, 2017. Available online at *learnersdictionary. com/definition/honor.*

9. Shaunti Feldhahn, *For Women Only* (Col- orado Springs, Colorado: Multnomah Books, 2013), 10.

10. Shaunti Feldhahn, "For Women Only Survey" *Shaunti.com* accessed on March 17, 2017. Available online at *shaunti.com/ wp-content/uploads/2014/01/For-Women- Only-Survey.pdf.*

11. Gary Thomas, "Cherish" *Gary Thomas blog* November 4, 2016, accessed on March 17, 2017. Available online at *garythomas.com/ cherishing.*

12. Shaunti Feldhahn, Jeff Feldhahn *For Men Only: A Straightforward Guide to the Inner Lives of Women* (Colorado Springs, Colo- rado: Multnomah Books, 2006), 156.

13. Oswald Chambers, *The Quotable Oswald Chambers* (Grand Rapids: Discovery House, 2008).

14. Charles Barnett, *Reflections in the Ripples: No-Wake Zone* (Bloomington, IN: Xlibris LLC, 2014), 599.

15. Ellie Lisitsa, "Apply the Research: Building Your Emotional Bank Account" *The Gottman Institute blog* February 15, 2013, accessed on March 17, 2017. Available online at *gottman.com/blog/ apply-the-research-building-your-emotional- bank-account.*

16. Gordon Edlin, Eric Golanty, Kelli McCor- mack Brown, *Essentials for Health and Wellness* (Sudbury, MA: Jones and Bartlett Publishers, 1997), 33.

17. Ibid, Hawkins.

18. Adapted from: James Dobson, "Real Love-Newsletter" *Dr. James Dobson's Family Talk ™* 2012 Available online at *drjamesdobson.org/news/commentaries/ real-love.*

19. Adapted from: David and Teresa Fer- guson, *Intimate Encounters* (Austin: Inti- macy Press, 1997), 52.

20. Ibid.

SESSION 5

1. Charles R. Swindoll, *Getting Through the Tough Stuff* (Nashville: Thomas Nelson, 2004), 89-90.

2. Justin Taylor, "Lewis on Love and God." *The Gospel Coalition blog* July 15, 2010, accessed March 15, 2017. Available online at *blogs.thegospelco- alition.org/justintaylor/2010/07/15/ lewis-on-love-and-god.*

3. "Understanding the Meaning of the Term 'Disciple'" *Bible.org*, accessed on March 15, 2017. Available online at *bible.org/ seriespage/2-understanding-meaning-term- disciple* © 2017 Bible.org

4. Gary Thomas, *Sacred Pathways* (Grand Rapids: Zondervan, 1996).

5. "Definition of busyness" *Merriam-Webster's Dictionary* Accessed May 2, 2017. Avail- able online via merriam-webster.com/ dictionary/busy.

6. Ibid, Thomas, *Sacred Pathways.*

7. Ibid, Thomas, *Sacred Pathways.*

8. Ibid, Thomas, *Sacred Pathways.*

9. Ibid, Thomas, *Sacred Pathways.*

10. Ibid, Thomas, *Sacred Pathways.*

11. Ibid, Thomas, *Sacred Pathways.*

12. Ibid, Thomas, *Sacred Pathways.*

13. Ibid, Thomas, *Sacred Pathways.*

14. Ibid, Thomas, *Sacred Pathways.*

SESSION 6

1. Robert Byrne, *The 2,548 Wittiest Things Anybody Ever Said* (New York: Touchstone, 2012).

2. Dennis Rainey and Barbara Rainey, *Moments Together for Couples: Devotions for Drawing Near to God and One Another* (Ventura, CA: Regal Books From Gospel Light, 1995), 9.

3. Ed Wheat and Gaye Wheat, *Intended for Pleasure* (Grand Rapids: Revell, 1977), 215-216.

4. Katherine M. Hertlein, Gerald R. Weeks, Nancy Gambescia, eds., *Systematic Sex Therapy, Second Edition* New York: Routledge, 2015), 55.

5. Ibid, Wheat.

6. Dr. Mehmet Oz, MD, "Q&A Achieving Orgasm" *ShareCare* Accessed on March 15, 2017. Available online at *sharecare.com/ health/achieving-orgasm/how-long-to-orgasm.*

7. Debby Herbenick, Ph.D., "10 Lessons About the Female Orgasm" *Men's Health,* April 27, 2015, accessed on March 15, 2017. Available online at *menshealth.com/ sex-women/10-lessons-about-female-orgasm.*

8. Shaunti Feldhahn, "For Men Only: National Survey of Women for For Men Only" *Shaunti.com* June 7, 2006, accessed on April 10, 2017. Available online at *shaunti.com/wp-content/uploads/2014/01/ FMO-Survey-Results.pdf.*

9. Ibid.

10. Juli Slattery, "Sex Is an Emotional Need," *Focus on the Family blog* 2009, accessed on March 15, 2017. Available online at *focusonthefamily.com/marriage/sex-and-intimacy/ understanding-your-husbands-sexual-needs/ sex-is-an-emotional-need#fn3.*

11. Juli Slattery, "Sex Is a Relational Need," *Focus on the Family blog* 2009, accessed on March 15, 2017. Available online at *focusonthefamily.com/marriage/sex-and-intimacy/ understanding-your-husbands-sexual-needs/ sex-is-a-relational-need.*

12. Douglas E. Rosenau, *A Celebration of Sex for Newlyweds* (Nashville: Thomas Nelson, Inc., 2002), 120.

13. James Strong, *Strong's Exhaustive Concordance of the Bible* accessed on March 15, 2017, via Blue Letter Bible. Available online at *blueletterbible.org/lang/lexicon/ lexicon.cfm?Strongs=G567&t=KJV.*

SESSION 7

1. Kevin Van Anglen, *Simplify, Simplify: And Other Quotations from Henry David Thoreau* (New York: Columbia University Press: 1996), 179.

2. Cathy A. Costantino and Christina Sickles Merchant, *Designing Conflict Management Systems: A Guide to Creating Productive and Healthy Organizations* (San Francisco: Jossey-Bass, 1996), xiii.

3. David K. Williams, "Top 25 Quotes To Discover The Leader In You" *Forbes.com* August 17, 2013, accessed on March 17, 2017. Available online at *forbes.com/sites/ davidkwilliams/2013/08/17/top-25-quotes-to-discover-the-leader-in-you/#296e34e431be.*

4. Howard J. Markman, Scott M. Stanley, and Susan L. Blumberg, *Fighting For Your Marriage* (San Francisco: John Wiley & Sons, Inc, 2010), 5.

5. Howard J. Markman, Scott M. Stanley, and Susan L. Blumberg, *Fighting For Your Marriage* (San Francisco: John Wiley & Sons, Inc, 1995), 4.

6. Ibid, Markman, Stanley, Blumberg, 1995, 5.

7. Ibid, Markman, Stanley Blumberg, 2010, 12.

8. Ron Biagini, *Does Anyone Speak Female?: A Guide to Unlocking Her Heart* (Mustang, Oklahoma: Tate Publishing & Enterprises, 2009), 260.

9. "The Smalley Institute Personality Test," accessed on March 17, 2017. Available online at *http://smalley.cc/images/Personality-Test.pdf*.

10. Barry Farber, *12 Cliches of Selling (and Why They Work)* (New York: Workman Publishing Company, Inc., 2001), 170.

11. Ibid, Smalley Institute

12. David L. Brown "Keep the Home Fires-Burning" *Logos Resource Page* 1990, accessed March 15, 2017. Available online at *logosresourcepages.org/Family/pres-mar.htm*.

13. Gabriella D. Filippi, *Celebrate Your Seasons: Inspirational Devotions to Progress in Love and Grace* (Lanhan, Maryland: Hamilton Books, 2011), 120.

14. Craig E. Runde, Tim A. Flanagan, *Becoming a Conflict Competent Leader: How You and Your Organization Can Manage Conflict Effectively, Second Edition* (San Francisco: Jossey-Boss, 2013), 1.

15. Jone Johnson Lewis, "Dorothy Thompson quotes," *ThoughtCo.* November 30, 2015, accessed on March 17, 2017. Available online at *thoughtco.com/dorothy-thompson-quotes-3530067*.

16. Ibid, Markman, Stanley Blumberg, 2010, 37.

17. Ibid, Markman, Stanley Blumberg, 2010, 42.

18. Ibid, Markman, Stanley Blumberg, 2010, 47.

19. Ibid, Markman, Stanley Blumberg, 2010, 57.

20. Ibid, Markman, Stanley Blumberg, 2010, 50.

21. Holly Hudson, "We Need to Talk" blog *Focus on the Family Africa blog* May 26, 2015, accessed on March 15, 2017. Available online at *safamily.co.za/we_need_to_talk*.

22. Dr. James Dobson, "Fundamentals of a Christian Marriage" *Dr. James Dobson's Family Talk™* accessed on March 15, 2017. Available online at *drjamesdobson.org/articles/pray-for-america/fundamentals-christian-marriage*.

23. Gary L. Thomas, *Sacred Marriage Gift Edition: Discover Your Soul's Path to God* (Grand Rapids: Zondervan, 2011), 48.

SESSION 8

1. John Steinbeck, *Travels with Charley: In Search of America* (New York: Penguin Books, 1962), 4.

2. Amanda Green, "14 of George Bernard Shaw's Most Brilliant Quotes." *Mental Floss* November 2, 2014, accessed on March 15, 2017. Available online at *mentalfloss.com/article/59813/14-george-bernard-shaws-most-brilliant-quotes*.

3. Maria Damanaki, "If you Want to Go Quickly, Go Alone. If You Want to Go Far, Go Together." *The Huffington Post blog* March 1, 2016, accessed on March 15, 2017. Available online at *huffingtonpost.com/maria-damanaki/if-you-want-to-go-quickly_b_9352480.html*.

4. H. Norman Wright, *Mothers, Sons and Wives* (Ventura, California: Regal Books, 1994).

5. Joseph Thayer, *Thayer's English-Greek Lexicon* (Peabody, MA: Hendrickson Publishers, 1995) via *mywsb.com*.

6. James Strong, *Strong's Exhaustive Concordance of the Bible*, accessed on March 15, 2017, via Blue Letter Bible. Available online at *blueletterbible.org/lang/lexicon/lexicon.cfm?Strongs=H5800&t=KJV*.

7. Larry D. Watson and Richard A. Hoefer, *Developing Nonprofit and Human Service Leaders: Essential Knowledge and Skills* (Los Angeles: Sage Publications, Inc., 2014), 65.

8. Ibid, H. Norman Wright, *Mothers, Sons and Wives*.

APPENDIX

1. Katie Reilly, "10 of Mother Teresa's Most Powerful Quotes" *Time.com* September 3, 2016, accessed on March 15, 2017. Available online at *time.com/4478287/mother-teresa-saint-quotes*.

NOTES

What's Next?

ESSENTIAL STUDIES FOR MARRIED COUPLES

THE 7 RINGS OF MARRIAGE
Jackie Bledsoe
8 Sessions

From the engagement ring to years after the wedding ring, every season of a marriage requires renewed commitment, fresh perspective, and practical biblical wisdom. Each of the 7 "rings" outlined in this study will teach couples to view their marriage with the end in mind, ultimately leading to a lasting and fulfilling relationship. The 7 Rings include: the Engagement RING (the beginning), the Wedding RING (the commitment), DiscoveRING (the real you), PerseveRING (the work), RestoRING (the fixing), ProspeRING (the goal), and MentoRING (the payback).

Bible Study Book   005753519 $12.99
Leader Kit   005644102 $79.99

LifeWay.com/7Rings

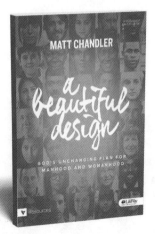

A BEAUTIFUL DESIGN
Matt Chandler
9 Sessions

God created us to function according to His perfect design, and for all of human history, our world has been male and female. But our ever-changing culture faces challenges due to sin. More than ever the church needs to be a safe refuge for the gender confused, the sexually broken, the single, the married, and the divorced. In this study, Matt Chandler gives evidence that God's plan for man and woman is the ultimate design. And life lived within this beautiful and unchanging design leads to our greatest joy.

Bible Study Book 005782093 $12.99
Leader Kit   005782094 $99.99

LifeWay.com/BeautifulDesign